THE
Artichoke
COOKBOOK

THE
Artichoke
COOKBOOK

PATRICIA RAIN

CELESTIALARTS

The recipes *Baked Stuffed Artichokes* and *Mrs. Fleichner's Stuffed Artichokes* from *American Cookery,* by James Beard. Copyright ©1972 by James Beard. By permission of Little, Brown and Company.

Textual quotations by James Beard appear from *American Cookery,* by James Beard. Copyright ©1972 by James Beard. By permission of Little, Brown and Company.

Textual quotation by Mrs. Grieve appears from *A Modern Herbal,* by Mrs. M. Grieve. Grieve, M., *A Modern Herbal,* Dover Publications, Inc., New York, 1971. Used by permission.

The recipe *Greek Pilaf Stuffed Artichokes* is from *The Moosewood Cookbook* by Mollie Katzen. Copyright 1977. Used with permission. Available from Ten Speed Press, P.O. Box 7123, Berkeley, CA 94707. $9.95 (paper), $12.95 (cloth) + $.75 for postage & handling.

The recipe *Artichoke Bottoms With Salmon Mousse* appears from *The Seasonal Kitchen* by Perla Meyers. Copyright ©1973 by Perla Meyers. Used by permission of Holt, Rinehart & Winston.

The recipes *Stuffed Artichokes* and *Artichoke Sauté With Mustard & Chives* appear from *New Almond Cookery,* by Michelle Schmidt. Copyright ©1984 by the California Almond Growers Exchange. Reprinted by permission of SIMON & SCHUSTER, Inc.

The recipes *Artichoke and Grapefruit Salad, Warm Salad of Curly Endive and Artichoke Hearts,* and *Artichoke Hearts with Melted Goat Cheese* appear from *Chez Panisse Menu Cookbook,* by Alice Waters. Copyright ©1983 by Alice Waters. Used with permission of Random House, Inc.

The quote by Angelo Del Chiaro is taken from the transcript of a taped interview done in 1979 of Angelo Del Chiaro by Brian Barsotti.

Many recipes were given to the author over the years, and I gratefully acknowledge the following individuals for their specific contributions to this book: Anna Anteater, Pati Boutonnet, Joe Carcione, Dina Collins, Ron & Lynn Duarte, Michael Jackson & The Moss Landing Oyster Bar and Company, Valerie Phipps, Joy Pieri, Sotere Torregian, and Dolores Tottino.

The majority of my research was collected from oral histories, anecdotes, folklore, and informative stories passed on to me by farmers, agricultural people, the California Artichoke Advisory Board, and various handouts/pamphlets collected at vegetable stands, festivals, and fairs. In every case I have made the best effort to credit the sources of information, particularly recipes. But of course, as Margaret Fox notes in her cookbook *Cafe Beaujolais,* there are now tens of thousands of cookbooks in print, a fact which makes the idea of a new, unique recipe almost an impossibility as recipes get traded, adapted, modified, and so on. If there is any duplicated recipe—or perhaps one that is so similar to another elsewhere—I offer my apologies in advance for not knowing. But every effort was made to properly credit recipes, and the others I consider to be my own—I have cooked them all and tasted them all, and because of their excellence, I offer them here.

Celestial Arts
P.O. Box 7327
Berkeley, CA 94707

First Printing, 1985

Cover image copyright © 1984 Batista Moon Studio

Made in the United States of America

Library of Congress Cataloging in Publication Data

Rain, Patricia, 1943–
    The artichoke cookbook.

    Bibliography: p.
    Includes index.
    1. Cookery (Artichokes)   I. Title.
TX803.A7R35 1985   641.6′532   85-5771
ISBN 0-89087-415-8 (pbk.)

5   —   96   95   94   93   92

CONTENTS

ACKNOWLEDGEMENTS

My gratitude and heartfelt thanks go to the many individuals and families along the California Coast who shared with me their colorful and exciting histories and experiences, and who donated recipes for this book, to Hank Sciaroni and Neal de Vos for providing technical data and research information, and to members of the Menlo Park Library staff. Special thanks to Pat Hopper of the Artichoke Advisory Board for her information, suggestions, support and good humor, and to Betty Martin for her assistance with the manuscript. And love and appreciation go to my companion, Robert, and my daughter, Serena, for their patience and willingness to spend a few months listening to artichoke stories and eating artichokes *several* times a week.

Patricia Rain

FOREWORD

A first encounter with an artichoke can be a perplexing and somewhat formidable experience, for the artichoke gives little clue from its appearance of the delights that wait within. The ideal artichoke has a smooth, leathery skin with tightly closed leaves or bracts that look almost like scales and are tipped at each end with a small, sharp spine. Its shape varies from spherical, to conical, to elipsoid, to ovoid. Depending on the variety, its color may be green tinged with reddish-purple tips, or it may be largely purple interspersed with streaks of green.

At peak harvest time it appears unripe, as if it should be placed on a window ledge to soften. Well displayed in a supermarket produce section, artichokes appear as if they would make a reasonable alternative to flowers for an unusual table centerpiece. Who would suspect at first glance that this novel looking so-called food would have any culinary value!

Fortunately, the paradox of the artichoke is that despite its almost other-worldly appearance, it is a marvelously delicious food. This book is designed for those of you who have never been served a well prepared artichoke, to introduce some of the many ways that artichokes can be enjoyed, but even veteran consumers of this sophisticated thistle will find some pleasant surprises for both the mind and palate on the pages that follow.

I encourage readers to approach these recipes as creatively as possible. A recipe is only a guideline which can usually be altered or modified somewhat without serious consequences. Eliminate or substitute herbs, vary the amount of garlic, add more wine or less cheese, add a tomato or pepper, or simply use a recipe as the basis of creating your own specialty. The only ingredient in the recipes that can't be substituted without changing the theme is the artichoke. Experiment by tasting while cooking, and allow yourself to imagine creative ways to enjoy this very special thistle.

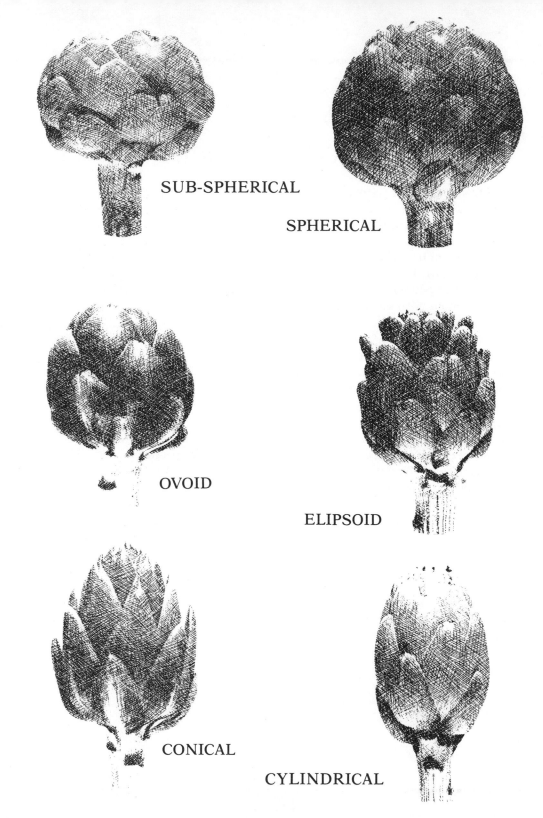

SUB-SPHERICAL

SPHERICAL

OVOID

ELIPSOID

CONICAL

CYLINDRICAL

A GALLERY OF THISTLES

The artichoke, known botanically as *Cynara Scolymus*, is a member of the *asteraccae (compositae)* family with a species cast of thousands. Some of the more familiar relatives are lettuce, sunflowers, asters, endive, chicory and thistles. Thistles are defined as any of various prickly plants of the *compositae* family, so artichokes are, technically, thistles.

The artichoke plant is a perennial that grows as much as six feet in diameter and to a height of three to four feet. The silvery-green leaves are long and arching, making it somewhat similar in appearance to a giant fern. If the flowerbud remains on the stalk, it produces a beautiful violet-purple flower about six to seven inches in diameter.

Although there are as many as 50 types of artichokes worldwide, only the *Green Globe* or Italian variety, is grown commercially in the United States. Color, shape and spininess vary significantly from variety to variety and even within a specific variety. Spherical, ovoid and elipsoid shapes are considered best for market; however, the cylindrical shape tends to be predominant. Artichokes in Italy often have reddish-purple or purple leaves. This is another predominant characteristic of the flowerbud that scientists have bred out of the *Green Globe*.

There is often confusion regarding the relationship of the globe artichoke, to the Jerusalem artichoke, Chinese artichoke, and cardoon.

The Jerusalem artichoke, *Helianthus tuberosus*, is distantly related to the globe artichoke, but its more direct lineage is with the sunflower family, its flowers turning to follow the sun. It is native to the North American plains of Canada and the United States, growing as far south as Arkansas and Georgia. Native Americans introduced it to the Europeans; Samuel de Champlain found the Indians raising them in the Cape Cod region in 1605. It was taken to Europe where it grew well. The Italians named it *Girasola articiocca*, or sunflower artichoke, as they felt the edible tuber had a similar flavor to the artichoke.

The Chinese artichoke is a member of the mint family, *Stachys sieboldii*, most closely related to Wood Betony. It is a native of North China, and other than producing an edible tuber, it has no similarity to either the globe or Jerusalem artichokes.

The cardoon, *Scolymus cardunculus*, is one of the three native wild plants of the Mediterranean and is considered by some botanists to be a variety of the globe artichoke, but probably the opposite is true.

The cardoon plant is taller than the artichoke, with varieties growing from 8 to 10 feet tall. The leaves are pale green, covered with silvery down, and are more serrated than artichoke leaves. The differences are well described by a 16th century gardener:

> *There be two kindes of Artechokes, the one (artichoke) with brode leaves and nothing prickley, the other (cardoon), whose leaves be all gashed full of sharpe prickles and deepe cuttes, which may be called the Thistell Artechoke.*

Cardoon flowers are often used instead of the artichoke flowers in commercial floral arrangements, fresh or dried, as the cardoon flower holds its shape better than the artichoke flower when processed. These flowers are gathered from plants that have gone wild through the hills of Benicia in the northeastern San Francisco Bay Area. Cardoon plants are cultivated for food by Italian families throughout California, and the midribs (also known as *cardone*) can be purchased at roadside stands and specialty markets.

In 1949 a publicity tour to promote Marilyn Monroe included a number of towns in the Salinas Valley and the Central California coast. In Castroville, the then unknown starlet was crowned Artichoke Queen. I asked Hugo Tottino about her visit.

Hugo didn't remember many of the details of the visit as it was so long ago. He did remember Randi Barsoti, who was at that time manager of the plant, taking her on a tour.

"There were about five of us younger guys all excited to meet her. She was real pretty, very nice, and she gave us each a kiss. I think I told her I hoped she'd make it big.

Oh, I do remember some of the older guys were too embarrassed to come meet her, especially Michelli. We tried to get him to come out, but he hid until she was gone. But we younger guys, you'd better believe we wanted to meet her. Sure."

And for the record: Yes, Marilyn Monroe liked artichokes.

ARTICHOKE HISTORY & LORE

EARLY HISTORY

There are three wild species of plants very similar to the artichoke plant as it is known today, growing in the central and western Mediterranean basin and Canary Islands, the Aegean Islands, and in southern Turkey, Syria, Lebanon, and Israel.

It is from these plants that people began to serve artichokes at their dining tables over 2,000 years ago. And while the artichokes of today were probably cultivated from the wild plants of Italy, the name itself came from the Arabic *Al Kharshuf*, and was brought by Moroccan invaders to Spain where the name was changed to *alcachofa*, and thence to Italy and *carciofa*. The artichokes that were served were described by writers of that time as being similar to asparagus.

There are two theories about artichoke evolution at that time. One is that what was then called "artichoke" was actually the young midribs of the plant, as the flowerbuds of these wild plants were small, spiny, and unpleasant to eat. The young midribs are fern-like in appearance and not dissimilar to asparagus ferns. The other theory is that the flowerbuds were in fact evolved enough for use, and the comparison to asparagus was made because the asparagus fiddlehead looked somewhat like the small artichoke flowerbuds.

Dioscordes, the Greek physician, wrote of artichokes around the time of the birth of Christ. By the time the Greeks and Romans were outdoing each other and undoing themselves with wild and excessive dining, the artichoke was an adored luxury item, forbidden to the commoners, preserved in honey and vinegar and seasoned with laserwort and cumin so that it could be served at any time of the year. The early Roman scholar and naturalist Pliny said that the artichoke was more esteemed and brought a higher price than any other garden herb.

With the fall of Rome, so fell the artichoke, remaining in obscurity until the 15th century. If indeed the early artichokes were actually the plant midribs, it is likely that during the Dark Ages the plants were transformed, through selective growing in monastery gardens, to the plants we know today, cultivated for the flowerbuds. Or they may simply have been selectively perfected to be of the quality and size of modern artichokes. Regardless, the artichoke made its grand debut in 1466 when one of the Strozzi family brought it from Florence to Naples. It was a rare commodity, greatly heralded by its devotees.

Rumor has it that Catherine de Medici introduced the artichoke to France, bringing it with her from Italy at the age of 14 when she crossed the Alps to marry Henry II. Catherine was a native of Tuscany where artichokes had been under cultivation for almost 50 years before her birth in 1519. However they arrived, artichokes were a grand success in France. Not so, however, when they were introduced to England in 1548—the British apparently preferring beef and ale to thistles. When it was served forth, it was well disguised with liquor, as this recipe from the *Compleat Cook*, printed for Obadiah Blagrave at the Sign of the Black Bear in St. Paul's Churchyard, 1655, demonstrates:

Boyl'd Artichocks
Take and boyl them in a Beef-Pot; when they are Tender sodden, take off the Tops, leaving the Bottoms with some round about them, then put them into a Pipkin, put some fayre Water to them, two or three spoonful of Sacke, a spoonful of sugar, and so let them boyle upon the Coals, still pouring on the liquor to give it a good Taste.

The first written record of artichokes in the United States was in *McMahon's Gardeners Catalogue* in 1806. Seeds were offered in catalogues in the early 19th century and featured two varieties. This venture was not successful, however, as artichoke plants grown from seeds frequently revert back to their wilder relatives and produce inedible buds.

In the mid-1800's French immigrants brought artichoke plants to Louisiana where the *Creole* artichoke was grown. The first commercial fields were developed in Louisiana, and artichokes were sent north to Chicago and New York, but by the 1940's these fields were all gone.

The history of this early Louisiana artichoke industry is shrouded in mystery. What little information I obtained about the *Creole* artichoke came from the Department of Agriculture at the University of Louisiana. Even the experts, however, have no definite knowledge of why the artichoke production ceased. It is assumed that it was no longer a profitable crop, as the plants only produced once a year in the South, but no one seems to know what happened to the fields of *Creole* artichokes or to the Cajun farmers who cared for them.

TODAY

In the late 19th century Italian immigrants began planting California's first commercial artichoke fields south of San Francisco, between San Pedro Valley and Moss Beach, just north of Half Moon Bay. By 1900 there were 500 acres of artichokes being cultivated along this coastal strip.

From Half Moon Bay farmers travelled south to San Gregorio, Pescadero, Davenport, Santa Cruz, and ultimately Castroville, at the edge of the fertile Salinas valley.

The artichoke industry first began in Castroville in 1922 when Angelo Del Chiaro and his cousin Dan rented land for $25 an acre complete with housing, packing sheds, roads, and electricity. They planted 150 acres in artichokes. In 1979 Del Chiaro said: "We had to go down to Half Moon Bay to get the plants . . . we plant it all . . . hundred fifty acres, 1921-1922. All artichokes. And we start to pick artichokes around May and June. Boy oh boy, you should've seen the artichokes. It is hard to believe. Nice, oh boy! They was like a tree, a tree, all full of artichokes."

By 1926 there were nearly 12,000 acres of artichokes under cultivation on the California coast. The acreage has fluctuated through the years, but it is currently just under 12,000 acres and has been since the 1940's.

It's not surprising that so many people in the United States are unfamiliar with artichokes because they are grown commercially in only four counties

on the California coast, and our farm output is quite small when compared to that of other countries. For instance, Italy has 150,000 acres under cultivation; Spain, 50 to 60,000 acres; France 35,000 acres; Argentina 19,000 acres; and Algeria 14,000 acres. Nearly 95% of the total world production of approximately 386,000 cultivated acres is grown in the countries bordering the Mediterranean Sea.

Regardless of the relatively low production of artichokes in the United States, opportunities to purchase and prepare artichokes—fresh or processed—are becoming increasingly easy, as improved methods of packing and shipping make them available year round in all metropolitan areas in the United States, and in some of the less populated areas as well. If you are unable to find artichokes in your area, request that your grocery store start carrying them, especially in the spring.

CULTIVATION

Artichokes have always been planted, cultivated and harvested by hand. Plants are started with a piece of root cut by knife, placed in a hole prepared with a shovel, and harvested by hand with a short, thick knife similar to a paring knife. The cut artichokes are thrown into heavy nylon or canvas packs that are worn on the back. The packs are dumped into large bins at the end of the rows. After the main harvest, the plants are cut back by hand with a "stumping iron" which looks like a large spatula with an offset handle.

Although artichokes are grown and harvested year round, the peak season is late March through May, with a smaller but important season in the fall. Each field may be picked 30 times a year.

In early June, most of the fields are cut back to prevent the plants from producing during the summer season, ensuring a larger fall and winter crop. Depending upon the soil, plants are divided every 4 to 8 years. All of this meticulous hand work brings a premium, quality crop—but it also is the reason why artichokes are seldom an "everyday" food like potatoes and carrots.

After harvesting, artichokes are taken to the packing houses where they are sorted on conveyer belts, boxed in waxed cartons to protect them from dehydration, and put into cold storage for shipping to the major markets across the country. Hydrocooling the artichokes when they first arrive from harvest has helped to keep the flowerbuds fresh for longer periods of time and to keep the artichokes from turning black. These improved methods of packing, storing, and shipping have affected the market favorably—the early farmer lost part of his harvest because of the inability to keep his produce fresh.

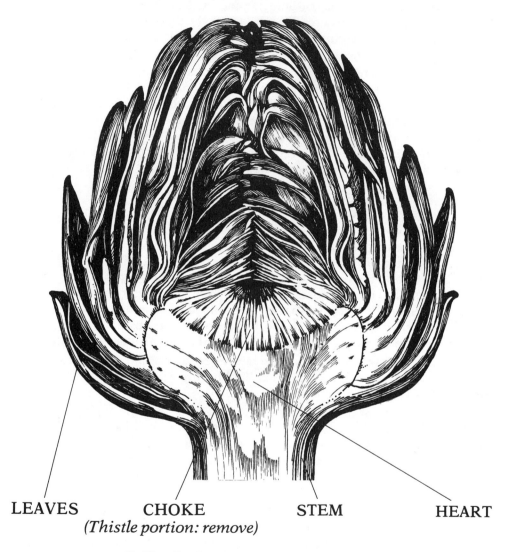

LEAVES   CHOKE   STEM   HEART
(Thistle portion: remove)

CROSS-SECTION
OF
ARTICHOKE

SELECTING & PREPARING ARTICHOKES

SELECTING ARTICHOKES

Choose artichokes that are bright green in color and have tightly closed leaves. Reject artichokes that feel or look dry or withered. In the late winter and early spring artichokes are sometimes bronze tinged or have slightly split or opened leaves. This is caused by light frosts, but produces artichokes with the best flavor due to the slow maturing process. Summer artichokes tend to have more open leaves, a more reddish-purple tinge, and longer spines than the winter and spring flowerbuds. Discard the outer leaves of summer artichokes before cooking, as they are often inedible.

Size is not an indication of quality or maturity. The largest flowerbuds grow on the center stalk with the smaller ones on the side branches, and with tiny but mature buds at the base of the plant. The largest are the best for stuffing or as a hot or cold entree, the medium for eating with sauces or for most recipes, and the smallest, sometimes the size of a large egg, for marinating and deep frying.

*Place Artichoks in Water cold with the Tops downwards
that all the Dust and Sand may boil out.*

18th Century Writer

PREPARATION

Wash artichokes in water, then cut off the stems at the base and remove the small bottom leaves and any that are discolored. Cut about 1 inch off the top, and trim off the thorny tips of each leaf with scissors (optional).

Place artichokes in a large pot and fill with enough water to cover the artichokes half-way. Add 1 tablespoon vinegar or lemon juice per quart of water, or add lemon slices. This acidulated water prevents the artichokes from darkening. Some additional flavorings are: olive oil (a couple of tablespoons per pot of water), garlic cloves, onions, marjoram, tarragon, bay leaves, rosemary sprigs, thyme or salt. Broth or wine can replace water, especially if artichokes are to be served plain. Do not use cast-iron or aluminum cooking utensils or non-stainless steel knives, as they will turn the artichokes black.

STORING ARTICHOKES

Store *fresh* artichokes unwashed in plastic bags in the refrigerator. They will keep approximately 2 to 3 weeks or longer.

To *freeze* artichokes, trim tops from buds. Rub cut surfaces with lemon. Cook the artichokes in acidulated water until they are cooked but still a little crunchy in texture. (Note: Do *not* freeze *uncooked* artichokes. They will turn brown when thawed, and the texture and taste will be bad. And remember a time-saving tip: artichokes can be stuffed before freezing.)

Once the artichokes are cooked for freezing, drain upside down thoroughly. Place artichokes upside down on a tray and freeze as quickly as possible in the coldest section of the freezer. When frozen through, remove briefly to place in plastic bags for longer freezer storage.

To thaw and cook frozen artichokes: Wrap each artichoke in tightly sealed aluminum foil. Place on a rack above boiling water. Cover and steam until cooked through.

BOILING & STEAMING

Cook artichokes 20 to 45 minutes, depending upon size. Artichokes are done when a knife or fork can be easily inserted into the base and the outside leaves pull off easily. If steaming artichokes, add about 10 to 20 minutes to the cooking time.

Specially designed "artichoke steamer racks" are available from many kitchenware stores. These racks support the artichoke upright in your steaming kettle so that only the tough stems remain immersed in boiling water.

MICROWAVING

To prepare artichokes in a microwave, soak them first in water 20 to 30 minutes to soften. See paragraph on preparation, then place artichokes upside down in a small amount of acidulated water. Cover with plastic wrap, pricking wrap in several places to allow steam to escape. To calculate cooking time, weigh artichokes in ounces and divide the weight in half to figure cooking time in minutes. Or, cook 6 to 8 minutes depending upon size, then allow artichokes to stand 5 minutes or until the bottoms are tender.

ARTICHOKE HEARTS & BOTTOMS

Artichoke *hearts* are comprised of the pale green inner leaves and the firm-fleshed base of artichokes. Use the smallest artichokes available. Remove the leaves until the light green ones appear. Cut off the top and stem. Put the hearts into acidulated water until ready for cooking. For salads and marinating, cook in boiling water until tender, drain, and cover with vinaigrette or other sauce. For deep frying, keep in acidulated water until almost ready to cook. Wrap in a towel to dry before dipping in batter. Larger artichokes can be used if necessary, just cut the hearts into quarters. Remove the furry center "choke" if artichoke hearts are cut, but leave the pale green leaves intact.

Artichoke *bottoms* are the firm-fleshed base of the artichoke with *all* the leaves and center choke removed. Use the largest artichokes available. Cook until tender, then remove all leaves and "choke" after cooking to prepare for stuffing.

Both artichoke hearts and bottoms can be purchased canned or frozen. If they have been canned or bottled in brine, rinse well before using.

CASINGS FOR STUFFING

Prepare artichokes in the same manner as for steaming or boiling. When tender, drain and allow to cool until easy to handle. Turning the artichoke upside down, press firmly while turning artichoke slightly clockwise. This will help to force the leaves open. Carefully remove inside leaves and the furry center "choke," spreading the outside leaves slightly to allow maximum space for filling the artichoke. Continue preparation for hot or cold entree.

ARTICHOKE PULP

Boil or steam large artichokes until tender. Remove leaves and scrape "meat" from the end of each leaf. Remove the chokes from the artichoke bottoms, then cut the bottoms in small pieces and run through a blender or food processor until smooth. Six large artichokes will make about 1-1/2 cups pulp. Many of the grower's wives use the culls for pulp. If artichokes have been in the refrigerator too long and the leaves have dried, the bottoms can still be used either for pulp or for filling with hot or cold foods.

SERVING PLATTERS

A number of potters have produced platters specially designed to serve artichokes. From the fanciful to the elegant, these dishes usually have a place for the leaves and a dish in the center for dipping the meaty leaves and hearts.

Among the more attractive platters I encountered were those made by Gloria Perezdiaz, proprietor and craftswoman of *Pottery en Español*. Her artichoke platters were designed especially for the Artichoke Festival in Castroville. For more information about the platters, write to: *Pottery en Español*, 1505 Tulare Street, Madera, CA 93637.

OTHER KITCHENWARE TOOLS

Many kitchenware shops stock myriad useful items for the home cook, but cooks in outlying areas often don't have access to well stocked stores (or, even in cities, kitchenware shops can be very specialized).

One of the best source books available for finding useful—and sometimes very rare and unique—kitchen tools is the *Whole Earth Access Mail Order Catalog*. This catalog lists hundreds of items for the cook, including the special artichoke steaming rack.

The catalog can be ordered directly from the publisher: Ten Speed Press, P.O. Box 7123, Berkeley, CA 94707. $11.95 postpaid.

NUTRITIVE VALUE

Artichokes are rich in iodine, a nutrient not found in most foods. They are also potassium rich, containing about 310 mg. of potassium per 100 gram serving of the edible portion. Artichokes rank 7th among fruits and vegetables in vitamin and mineral content, and they are a good source of vitamins A, B, and C.

The best news about artichokes is that they are a dieter's delight. Artichokes contain almost no fat, are very low in sodium, and there are only about 50 calories per one medium sized flowerbud. That, together with the time it takes to eat, makes the artichoke ideal for weight watchers—at least if the *Bernaise* sauce is passed over in favor of the *Vinaigrette*.

Mrs. M. Grieve, in A Modern Herbal, *states simply of artichokes, "The flowers are very handsome, and are said to possess the property of coagulating milk."*

Waverly Root, in Food, *says more directly, "The flowers of the artichoke curdle milk."*

SAUCES

The mere mention of artichokes instantly brings to mind images of succulent, steaming leaves and hearts dipped in rich and delicious sauces.

The recipes throughout this book provide a variety of ways to incorporate artichokes with other ingredients to create special dishes. For the most part these are recipes you will use when artichokes are plentiful, when you have time for experimenting with ways to prepare them, or when you want to make something unusual and unique.

Most of the time, however, artichokes are served steamed or boiled with dipping sauces on the side. A well-sauced artichoke will enhance any meal from the simple to the sublime.

This chapter, then, presents recipes for sauces that can be used for dipping artichoke leaves and hearts. A few, like *Bagna Cauda*, *Aioli*, and the three *Remoulade* sauces, are magnificent as dipping sauces for a variety of other fresh vegetables or even shrimp or crab. Make a platter and serve along with the artichokes.

The *Bechamel* and *Mornay* sauces could be used for dipping but are most often used to bind and enhance the ingredients in baked dishes.

I hope you'll experiment with the sauces to determine new ways to dress up artichokes for yourself and family or friends. If time permits, it's nice to have 2 or 3 sauces available to provide different flavors and textures. One or two large artichokes served with several sauces, hot crusty bread, and perhaps a glass of wine, can be a completely satisfying meal, one that you will likely want to repeat again and again.

BUTTER SAUCES

Melted butter with a squeeze of fresh lemon is a standard dipping sauce for artichokes. There are a number of variations on this basic sauce that are simple to prepare and that enhance the flavor of boiled or steamed artichokes. Combining a couple of the butter sauces could even be more delicious.

The variations that follow are based on 1/4 pound butter, either sweet or salted. Increase or decrease the recipes to suit your needs. Makes about 1/2 to 3/4 cup sauce.

Butter sauces can be served two ways. The first is to melt the butter, add the additional ingredients, and serve warm. The other is to use softened butter, blend in the additional ingredients, then whip slightly with a hand mixer or whisk. Chill butter and serve cold.

GARLIC BUTTER

Add up to 4 cloves of minced or pressed fresh garlic, or use 1 to 2 teaspoons garlic powder.

ANCHOVY BUTTER

Add 1 teaspoon anchovy paste and lemon juice to taste.

SALMON BUTTER

Grind or finely mince about 3 tablespoons fresh or smoked salmon or other fish. Add lemon juice to taste.

CAPER OR CAVIAR BUTTER

Add up to 3 tablespoons black or red caviar or 2 tablespoons chopped capers to butter. Add lemon juice to taste.

HERBED BUTTER

Use any of the following herbs or blend two or more together: 1 tablespoon fresh tarragon leaves, minced, 1/4 cup minced parsley, 2 to 3 tablespoons chopped fresh basil leaves, 1 tablespoon fresh dill, thyme or chervil, or 1 teaspoon fresh rosemary.

ADDITIONAL BUTTER SAUCE IDEAS

Fruit-flavored, balsamic or wine-flavored vinegars can be used instead of lemon juice in butter sauces. Butter can also be cooked until brown with 1/4 cup white wine or 1 tablespoon lemon juice or vinegar added. Season to taste with salt, pepper, garlic powder, Worcestershire sauce or Tabasco.

VINEGAR DRESSINGS

Vinegar can be used alone as a dipping sauce or as a dressing over artichokes. Balsamic and fruit-flavored vinegars impart a special flavor, or add herbs to a simple wine vinegar.

If vinegar alone is too tart, make a vinaigrette sauce.

BASIC VINAIGRETTE

1/2 cup wine vinegar
1 teaspoon salt
dash of pepper
1-1/2 cups olive oil (or salad oil)
1 tablespoon Dijon style mustard
lemon juice (optional)

Mix in a jar: wine vinegar, salt, dash pepper, and oil.

For a more piquant vinaigrette, add up to 1 tablespoon mustard. Lemon juice can be substituted for vinegar or used in combination.

Add garlic, minced or pressed, and herbs to taste.

Homemade mayonnaise is quite easy to make if a blender, food processor, or electric mixer is used. The secret to good mayonnaise is to add the oil to the egg-vinegar mixture slowly and in a steady stream.

HOMEMADE MAYONNAISE

2 large eggs
1 additional egg yolk (optional)
1 teaspoon Dijon style mustard
1 tablespoon wine vinegar (or 1 tablespoon lemon juice)
2 cups salad oil

Put eggs (or eggs and 1 egg yolk), mustard, wine vinegar or lemon juice (or a mixture of both), into a blender, and beat at high speed until well blended.

With the motor still on, add salad oil, a few drops at a time, adding oil a little more rapidly as oil is absorbed. Stop the blender a couple of times to stir mixture.

As the mixture thickens, an emulsion forms. The emulsion can break if overbeaten and will appear as if it has curdled or will become thin. If this happens, pour the emulsion into a bowl, clean blender, add an egg and a little vinegar, and then slowly pour broken emulsion back into blender until thickened.

Add more lemon juice or vinegar if desired, and salt and pepper to taste.

This recipe makes 2 to 2-1/2 cups mayonnaise.

MUSTARD MAYONNAISE

Add 1 to 2 teaspoons Dijon style mustard to 1/2 cup homemade mayonnaise. Add pressed garlic if desired.

GARLIC MAYONNAISE

Add as many cloves of pressed garlic as desired to mayonnaise while preparing it, or use the Aioli recipe on page 35 .

ANCHOVY MAYONNAISE

To make this interesting variation, you can try two different methods:
Add 1/2 to 1 teaspoon anchovy paste to 1/2 cup homemade mayonnaise.
Or, using one 2-oz. can of anchovies, mix the oil from the can into 1 cup of homemade mayonnaise, then add anchovies, finely minced.

CURRY MAYONNAISE

To make this special sauce, add 1 teaspoon curry powder to 1 cup homemade mayonnaise.
Or you can add a mixture of 1/4 teaspoon turmeric, 1/4 teaspoon coriander, and 1 teaspoon cumin to 1 cup homemade mayonnaise.

HERB MAYONNAISE

Add tarragon leaves, fresh thyme, dill, chervil, or finely minced parsley or basil leaves to mayonnaise. A combination of several herbs might be very nice.
Adding up to 1 tablespoon prepared pesto sauce to 1 cup mayonnaise creates an excellent dipping sauce, or use the following recipe for *Al Pesto Mayonnaise*.

AL PESTO MAYONNAISE

1 cup mayonnaise
2 tablespoons pine nuts
(or walnuts)
1/2 to 1-1/2 cloves garlic,
pressed
1/2 cup fresh basil leaves
2 sprigs fresh thyme (or 1/4
teaspoon dried thyme)
3/4 cup fresh parsley
1/4 cup milk (or olive oil)

Blend until smooth in a blender or food processor mayonnaise, pine nuts, garlic, basil, thyme, parsley, and milk (or olive oil).
Chill.

The following two classic dressings are always appropriate and delicious.

GREEN GODDESS DRESSING

1 clove garlic, minced or pressed

1/4 cup parsley, coarsely chopped

watercress

1 teaspoon dry tarragon

1 teaspoon anchovy paste (or finely chopped anchovy fillets)

2 teaspoons lemon juice

1 cup mayonnaise

In a blender or food processor, place garlic, parsley, green onions and watercress. Add salt, tarragon, anchovy paste (or fillets), and lemon juice.

Whirl until finely chopped.

Stir in mayonnaise.

Makes about 1-1/2 cups.

CLASSIC LOUIS DRESSING

1 cup homemade mayonnaise

1/4 cup tomato based chili sauce

1/4 cup green pepper, finely chopped

1/4 cup green onions, including tops, sliced

1/4 cup whipping cream

lemon juice to taste

In small bowl combine: mayonnaise, chili sauce, pepper, and green onions.

Whip the cream and fold it into the mixture. Add salt and lemon juice to taste.

Makes about 1-1/2 cups.

AIOLI SAUCE

12 to 16 large cloves garlic, pressed or minced
yolk of 1 hard cooked egg
2 teaspoons Dijon style mustard
2 raw whole eggs
4 tablespoons lemon juice
2 tablespoons salad oil
2 cups olive oil
salt to taste

In a mixing bowl or blender combine garlic, hard cooked egg yolk, mustard, raw eggs, and 2 tablespoons lemon juice.

Mix together with a fork or run on low speed until well blended.

Beat in salad oil, a few drops at a time, until creamy and yellow, using an electric mixer or blender.

Then beat in remaining 2 tablespoons lemon juice.

Gradually add olive oil, pouring in a thin stream while beating contantly, and add salt to taste.

This is a *Hollandaise* sauce recipe that I have used for years. I consider it almost "no-fail" and like it also because it uses whole eggs. Oil can be substituted for up to 1/2 the butter called in the recipe.

HOLLANDAISE SAUCE

8 tablespoons butter
juice of 1 lemon
1 tablespoon water
2 eggs
salt and pepper to taste

In a heavy 1 quart saucepan, melt butter. Add the lemon juice and tablespoon water.

In a small bowl beat eggs with a whisk, then slowly pour into the butter-lemon mixture, stirring constantly with a whisk.

As soon as sauce begins to thicken, turn off heat, beating until thick. Add salt and pepper to taste.

This sauce can be made an hour ahead and warmed to serve. Add a few drops of hot water when warming. If the sauce should curdle it can be saved by adding a tablespoon of hot water and beating with a whisk as it is warmed over low heat.

This recipe can be halved or doubled.

Bernaise sauce is a variation of sorts on *Hollandaise*. In case of disaster, it can be corrected in the same way as *Hollandaise*, by adding a tablespoon of hot water and beating with a whisk while warming over low heat.

BERNAISE SAUCE

1/4 cup wine vinegar or dry white vermouth

1 tablespoon shallots, minced (or green onions, minced)

3 tablespoons fresh tarragon, minced (or 1 tablespoon tarragon and 2 tablespoons parsley, minced)

1/8 teaspoon pepper

1/3 cup butter

2 whole eggs

pinch of salt

In a heavy 1 quart saucepan, boil vinegar (or vermouth) with shallots (or green onions), 1 tablespoon tarragon (or you may substitute 1/2 tablespoon of dried tarragon leaves), pepper, and a pinch of salt.

Pour off and discard all but 2 tablespoons of this boiled mixture.

In same saucepan, melt butter.

Beat eggs and add to melted butter. Add 2 tablespoons tarragon or parsley. Beat until thick with a whisk.

Remove from heat as soon as thickened.

CREAM CHEESE BERNAISE

2 tablespoons tarragon
vinegar
2 tablespoons green
onions, minced
1/4 teaspoon tarragon
2 3-oz. packages chive-
flavored cream cheese
1/3 cup fresh Parmesan
cheese, grated
2 tablespoons lime juice
1 teaspoon cream or milk

In a small saucepan boil tarragon vinegar with green onions and tarragon until vinegar is evaporated.

Combine onion mixture with cream cheese, Parmesan cheese, and lime juice.

Mash with a fork until smoothly blended.

Thin to a consistency that can be dipped but is not runny by adding 1 teaspoon cream or milk at a time until the desired thickness is reached.

Makes about 1 cup.

GREEK LEMON-EGG SAUCE

1-1/2 teaspoons cornstarch
dissolved in 1-1/2
teaspoons water
3/4 cup boiling water
1 egg
1 egg yolk
3 tablespoons lemon juice

Stir cornstarch dissolved in water into boiling water. Boil for 1 minute.

Beat 1 egg plus 1 egg yolk until light. Add fresh lemon juice, beating constantly.

Gradually pour hot liquid into egg-lemon mixture, beating constantly with wire whisk.

Return to pan and heat gently until slightly thickened. *Do not boil.*

This recipe can be doubled.

SOUR CREAM SAUCES

Using sour cream as a base, parsley, tarragon, chervil, basil or thyme leaves can be finely chopped and added.

Add 1 tablespoon lemon juice per cup of sour cream and either salt or soy sauce to taste.

Add 1/4 to 3/4 teaspoon horseradish to each cup of sour cream for a piquant sauce, or 1/3 cup finely chopped toasted almonds or pine nuts for a slightly crunchy sauce.

Anchovy paste can also be used in the same way as in mayonnaise. Experiment. Mix 2 or 3 different ingredients and try, adding more seasonings if necessary.

Here are two different recipes for the Southern favorite, *Remoulade* sauce. The first is quite simple. The next is more complex but also more flavorful. Use just for the artichokes, or make a special dish using shrimp, lobster or crab with artichokes on a bed of soft lettuce, and pour the sauce over all.

BASIC REMOULADE SAUCE

3 hard boiled egg yolks
1 raw egg yolk
3 teaspoons Dijon style mustard
1/4 teaspoon ground mace
2 teaspoons anchovy paste
2 teaspoons parsley, minced
2 teaspoons chives, minced
freshly ground pepper to taste
1 cup olive oil
1/4 cup tarragon vinegar
salt to taste

Mix the yolks of hard boiled eggs, raw egg yolk, mustard, mace, anchovy paste, parsley, chives, and pepper to taste.

Gradually add olive oil, beating with whisk until it begins to thicken.

Add tarragon vinegar, slowly, continuing to beat. When thickened, add salt to taste.

REMOULADE SAUCE
LE RUTH'S

1/4 cup wine vinegar

1/4 cup Creole mustard (recipe below)

2 tablespoons Hungarian paprika

1 tablespoon salt

1/2 to 1 teaspoon cayenne pepper

1-1/3 cups olive oil

1 cup scallions, including tops, minced

1/2 cup celery, minced

1/2 cup parsley, minced

FOR CREOLE MUSTARD:

1 tablespoon prepared mustard

2 teaspoons flour

2 teaspoons dry English mustard

2 teaspoons fresh horseradish, grated

2 teaspoons white pepper

1 teaspoon sugar

dash of celery salt

dash of salt

2/3 cup boiling water

Make Creole mustard (recipe below).

In a bowl beat together vinegar, Creole mustard, Hungarian paprika, salt, and cayenne pepper.

Add olive oil in a stream, 1/3 cup at a time, whisking, and continue to whisk the mixture until smooth.

Stir in scallions, celery, and parsley.

Chill the sauce, covered, for at least three hours.

CREOLE MUSTARD:

In a small saucepan combine prepared mustard, flour, dry English mustard, horseradish, and white pepper, sugar, and dashes of celery salt and salt.

Stir in boiling water and cook mixture over moderate heat until smooth and thickened.

Makes about 1/4 cup mustard.

This is an unusual sauce, one that's a rich treat.

ANNA ANTEATER'S PECAN SAUCE

12 tablespoons butter
1/2 cup shelled pecans,
finely chopped
2 teaspoons white wine
vinegar

Melt butter in a heavy saucepan.

When butter is hot but not brown, add pecans, stirring until nuts are well coated with butter and very hot. Add at once vinegar and stir vigorously. The mixture will "boil and fume furiously."

When settled, pour into the centers of artichokes and serve at once.

This recipe is perfect served in a fondue pot or a heatproof container that can be brought to the dining table. If you are not using a fondue pot, reheat over stove periodically. It is especially nice served with sour-dough french bread or baguette to catch the drips as you eat or to dip into the sauce along with the artichokes. This recipe can be doubled.

BAGNA CAUDA

1/2 cup butter
1/4 cup olive oil
2 to 3 cloves garlic, minced
or pressed
1/4 teaspoon freshly
ground pepper
1 tablespoon lemon juice
one 2-oz. can of anchovies

In a heatproof container or fondue pot combine butter, olive oil, garlic, pepper, and lemon juice.

Drain oil from can of anchovies into the butter mixture.

Finely chop the anchovies and add to other ingredients.

Place over medium heat until butter has melted. Serve.

BECHAMEL SAUCE

3 tablespoons butter
2 tablespoons flour
1/8 teaspoon ground
nutmeg
1-1/2 cups milk (or 3/4 cup
heavy cream and 3/4 cup
artichoke broth)
salt and pepper to taste

In a heavy saucepan melt butter over medium heat.

Add flour and nutmeg. Cook, stirring, until mixture is bubbling.

Remove from heat and add milk (or the cream and artichoke broth substitute).

Bring to rolling boil, stirring. Season with salt and pepper.

MORNAY SAUCE

3 tablespoons butter
5 tablespoons flour
2 cups light cream
2 cups Gruyere, Monterey
Jack, or Swiss cheese,
grated
salt and pepper to taste
extra cream as necessary

In a heavy saucepan melt butter.

Add flour, mixing well with wooden spoon until mixture is pale gold and well blended.

Remove from heat and slowly add cream until well blended.

Return to heat and cook until thick. Add cheese, season with salt and pepper, and add a little more cream as needed.

SOY SAUCES

Add freshly pressed ginger, lemon juice, finely ground horseradish, *wasabi* (a Japanese horseradish), a small amount of sugar, or garlic (or a combination of two or more of the above) to a good quality soy sauce for a low calorie, flavorful dip. This is especially nice with french fried artichokes.

*The juice of the artichoke, pressed out before it blossomed, was said to restore the hair on the head even when the head was quite bald.
It was also said that eating either the thistle or the root of the plant, sodden with water, enabled the individual to drink excessively, bringing on a great desire to do just that.*

APPETIZERS

Castroville, California is the undisputed Artichoke Center of the World, as proclaimed on a large sign hanging over the center of the town's main street, and each September the town becomes the lively seat of the annual Artichoke Festival.

The festival began in 1959 with a parade and barbeque and the crowning of the first Artichoke Festival Queen. There was an earlier Artichoke Queen, crowned in 1949 by a couple of growers who appreciated beauty in women as well as their plants. The queen? Marilyn Monroe.

On a Friday evening, in September, the festival begins with a dinner, dance, and crowning of one of the local contestants as the new Artichoke Queen. On Saturday and Sunday there are races, contests, a pancake breakfast, parade, an arts and crafts fair, continuous music—and of course plenty of food, including the french fried artichokes for which Castroville is famous.

In July the contestants for Artichoke Queen are introduced and the events leading to the festival are begun at an evening event where the wives of local growers serve artichoke appetizers and wine. One favorite is:

ARTICHOKE NIBBLES

2 jars marinated artichoke hearts
1-1/2 cups onions, minced
1 to 2 cloves garlic, minced
4 eggs
1/4 cup dry breadcrumbs
1/4 teaspoon dried oregano, crumbled
1/4 teaspoon hot pepper sauce
salt and pepper to taste
2 cups cheddar cheese, grated (or 1 cup cheddar cheese, grated, and 1 cup muenster cheese, grated)
3 tablespoons parsley, minced

Preheat oven to 325 degrees.

Grease a 7 × 11-inch baking pan.

In a medium skillet over medium heat, warm marinade from jars of artichoke hearts. Sauté the onions and garlic in marinade until soft, about 5 minutes. Remove with slotted spoon and set aside.

In large bowl beat eggs. Stir in breadcrumbs, oregano, hot pepper sauce, and salt and pepper to taste.

Chop artichoke hearts and add to egg mixture. Stir in onions, cheese, and parsley. Mix well.

Pour batter into prepared pan. Cook until golden, about 30 minutes.

Cut into 1-inch squares and serve.

Artichoke Nibbles can be prepared one day ahead and reheated in a 325 degree oven for 10 minutes.

This recipe, for which Castroville is famous, comes from Dolores Tottino, wife of a second generation Castroville artichoke grower, and daughter of an early farm family. In addition to being served during the festival, the *Giant Artichoke*—a large green plaster artichoke with attached buildings that include a restaurant, produce section, and gift store—features baskets of the fried hearts.

FRIED ARTICHOKES

1 quart oil
10 artichokes
1 egg
1/2 cup milk
1 teaspoon salt
1/2 teaspoon garlic salt
1/2 cup flour
1/2 cup Bisquick
1/2 teaspoon baking powder
2 tablespoons onion, chopped
2 tablespoons parsley, chopped (or 2 tablespoons parsley flakes)

Heat oil for deep frying in a wok, heavy saucepan, or deep fryer to 350 degrees.

Clean and trim artichokes and prepare as for hearts. Cut in halves or quarters, depending upon size. Set aside.

PREPARE BATTER: Beat egg and milk. Continue beating and add salt, garlic salt, flour, Bisquick, and baking powder. Stir in onion and parsley.

Add prepared artichoke pieces to batter. If batter seems too thin, add a little flour.

Deep fry in hot oil, turning artichoke pieces until they are browned. Drain on paper towels. Sprinkle with salt if desired.

The following recipe is my own adaptation of a classic favorite for fried artichokes. Dina Collins, owner of the Florentine Pasta Shop and Restaurant has told me always to use beer in the batter as it makes it very light. She must be right, as this batter is as light and delicate as good Japanese *tempura*. You can double or halve this recipe.

PATRICIA RAIN'S FRIED ARTICHOKES

1 quart oil
18 small artichokes
2 cups flour
1/4 teaspoon salt
2 cups beer
1 lemon
2 egg whites
1/4 cup oil

Clean and trim artichokes and prepare as for hearts. Cut in halves or quarters, depending on size, and immerse in a bowl of cold water into which the lemon juice has been squeezed.

PREPARE BATTER: Into a medium bowl measure flour and make a well in the center. Mix beer and 1/4 cup oil and pour into the well. Gently incorporate the flour into the liquid mixture with a whisk, stirring in one direction only, until batter is smooth. If possible, let the batter rest for 2 hours.

To fry artichokes, heat 1 quart oil for deep frying in a wok, heavy saucepan, or deep fryer to 350 degrees.

Make final preparations for the batter: Beat egg whites to soft peaks and gently fold them into the batter. Once this step is done, the batter can stand at room temperature for about 15 minutes.

Drain the artichoke hearts and dry well. Dip them into the batter and then gently drop them into the hot oil. Let batter set for about 30 seconds as they fry, then turn the artichokes until they are golden brown. Hint: Fry in small batches to allow the oil to return to 350 degrees before frying the next batch.

Italian families make a dish called *Frito Misto*. Using either of the batter recipes above, include any of the following with the artichokes: small whole cleaned mushrooms; flowerettes of cauliflower or broccoli (cut, if necessary); carrot sticks; rounds or sticks of zucchini or other summer squashes; thin slices of sweet potato; or onion rings.

Serve fried artichoke hearts or the *Frito Misto* "combination" as shown above with Parmesan cheese sprinkled over the freshly fried pieces, or with homemade mayonnaise, soy sauce, lemon butter, or another sauce of your choice (see *Sauce* section for recipes).

Pati Boutonnet, a Castroville grower's wife, serves this attractive dish, opening the cooked artichoke leaves into the shape of a sunflower. Some variations on this recipe include using cream cheese *Bernaise, Hollandaise,* or mayonnaise (see *Sauce* section for recipes). Paté or mousse or a prepared cheese spread can also be used.

PATI BOUTONNET'S ARTICHOKE SUNFLOWER

1 large artichoke
1 3-oz. package cream cheese
1/4 teaspoon garlic powder
1/4 teaspoon onion powder
1/4 teaspoon hot pepper seasoning
approximately 2 tablespoons milk or cream
1/4 pound small cooked shrimp

Clean, trim, and cook artichoke and remove all leaves. Set aside those leaves that are firm enough to handle and which have a good edible portion on the ends. Cut heart into quarters.

Blend cream cheese, garlic powder, onion powder, hot pepper seasoning, and enough milk or cream to make a smooth paste (about 2 tablespoons). Adjust seasoning.

Spread filling on the tip of each reserved leaf. Place 1 small shrimp on top of filling, and dust with paprika. Arrange leaves in concentric circles on a round tray to resemble an open sunflower. Place cut artichoke hearts in the center of the leaves, with more filling and shrimp. Serve.

I created this delicious spread for the wedding of some friends. It is an excellent way to serve something elegant while also using up slightly stale bread. Trim crusts from bread, cut into squares or rectangles, butter lightly, and toast in a slow oven until crisp. Spread with artichoke-cream cheese mix, sprinkle with paprika, and garnish with green and/or black olive slices and parsley. Crackers can be used instead of toast. This spread covers about 18 pieces of bread (or 36 toast rectangles).

ARTICHOKE-CREAM CHEESE SPREAD

1 jar marinated artichoke hearts
4 scallions
1/4 cup fresh parsley
6 sprigs of thyme
8-oz. cream cheese (soft-spreading, low fat if possible)
1/2 cup sour cream
2 cloves garlic, pressed
salt and pepper to taste
squeeze of lemon juice
1/2 cup walnuts, sunflower seeds, or almonds, chopped

Drain and save the marinade from artichoke hearts.* Chop the artichoke hearts finely with scallions, parsley, thyme, and leaves stripped from stems. Set aside.

Mix cream cheese with sour cream, garlic, salt and pepper to taste, and squeeze of lemon juice.

Add the chopped artichoke/onion/herb mixture to cream cheese, and add chopped nuts. Blend well. Adjust seasonings to taste.

Note: Always save marinade for other possible uses.

This recipe makes good use of artichoke leaves and stems when the artichoke bottoms have been used for another recipe. Use cooked leaves or cook raw leaves to make the paté. Whole artichokes can be used if preferred.

ARTICHOKE PATÉ

This recipe is divided into two parts. In order to make artichoke paté, you will need to prepare artichoke pulp or "meat," which is then blended with the necessary ingredients to create the delicious paté.

For making artichoke meat you will need:
artichoke leaves and stems from 6 to 8 artichokes (or more, depending on the amount you want to make).

4 to 5 quarts artichoke, vegetable, or chicken broth (artichoke broth can be saved by conserving the water in which you cook artichokes or hearts).

To make the paté, for each cup of mashed artichoke meat you will need:

1/2 cup cooked ham, minced (or 1/2 cup cooked chicken, minced)
3 tablespoons mayonnaise
3 tablespoons sour cream
1 teaspoon Worcestershire sauce
2 cloves garlic, minced or pressed
freshly ground pepper to taste

TO MAKE THE ARTICHOKE MEAT:

Put rinsed leaves and stems plucked from artichokes in a 5 to 6 quart kettle. Add broth. Cover, bringing to a boil, then simmer until stems are tender when pierced, about 20 minutes.

Uncover, remove from heat, and let cool. Remove leaves from broth. Scrape off meat and reserve. Discard leaves.

On stems, trim off fibrous exterior and mash into pulp. Blend meat from leaves with pulp from stems and measure.

TO MAKE THE PATÉ:

For each cup of mashed artichoke blend in measures as given above of ham, mayonnaise, sour cream, Worcestershire, garlic, and pepper.

Serve, or cover and chill up to 2 days. Scoop onto crackers.

The following recipe is good for a large party. Make 1 day ahead, then warm to serve.

ARTICHOKE BALLS

1 14-oz. can artichoke hearts packed in water

1 jar marinated artichoke hearts

2 eggs

1 tablespoon garlic juice

1 tablespoon Worcestershire sauce

1/2 to 1 teaspoon liquid smoke

1/2 teaspoon Tabasco sauce

1-1/2 cups Italian seasoned breadcrumbs

Grated Parmesan or Romano cheese

Drain the canned artichoke hearts (packed in water) and finely chop. Drain (but save the marinade) the marinated artichoke hearts and finely chop. Set aside.

In a large bowl, beat eggs with the saved marinade and blend with garlic juice, Worcestershire, liquid smoke, and Tabasco.

Add all the finely chopped artichoke hearts and breadcrumbs. Blend well.

Form into little balls and roll each ball in the grated cheese. Refrigerate.

Serve at room temperature or place on a lightly greased baking sheet and bake 7 to 10 minutes at 300 degrees. Serve immediately.

Artichoke balls can be refrigerated up to 1 week. Makes 60 to 80 balls.

This is special—nice for a small gathering.

SHRIMP SAGANAKI

1 pound raw medium-sized shrimp

10 to 12 small artichokes cut in half (or 1 package frozen artichoke hearts)

4 tablespoons olive oil

2 cloves garlic, pressed

1/2 teaspoon oregano, crumbled

salt and pepper to taste

2 tablespoons lemon juice

2 tablespoons parsley, finely chopped

Peel and devein shrimp. Prepare small artichokes as for artichoke hearts, cut in half, and cook for about 4 minutes or until barely cooked. (Or cook frozen artichoke hearts in boiling water for 2 minutes, then drain.)

Heat olive oil in a frying pan, adding shrimp and small whole mushrooms, and cook, stirring, until shrimp turn pink.

Add artichoke hearts, pressed garlic, oregano, and salt and pepper to taste. Heat until thoroughly warm.

Sprinkle with lemon juice and parsley, and stir lightly to blend.

Shrimp Saganaki can be served with toothpicks as an appetizer, or as a main dish served over rice. If serving over rice, add 2 tablespoons butter.

The following recipe can be also used as a side dish or light entree.

ARTICHOKE SPINACH SQUARES

2 to 3 fresh artichoke bottoms (or 1 package frozen artichokes)
1 bunch fresh spinach (or 1 package frozen spinach)
2/3 cup brown rice
4 eggs
2/3 cup milk
2 tablespoons butter
2 tablespoons onion, chopped
2 tablespoons parsley, chopped
1 teaspoon seasoned salt
freshly ground pepper
2 cups cheddar cheese, shredded

Preheat oven to 325 degrees.

Cook fresh artichoke bottoms (or frozen artichokes) and chop.

Cook spinach (fresh or frozen), drain, and chop.

Cook brown rice. While cooking, melt butter, then beat eggs with milk and add melted butter, chopped onion, parsley, seasoned salt, and pepper. Mix well.

Stir in rice with spinach, artichokes, and cheese.

Turn into a greased 9-inch cooking dish, and bake 30 to 45 minutes. Cut into squares before serving.

ADDITIONAL APPETIZER IDEAS

Artichoke hearts can be marinated with small mushrooms and cherry tomatoes and either speared with toothpicks or served on an antipasto platter with caper-covered marinated tuna, anchovies, olives, pickled vegetables, and meats and cheeses.

Artichoke hearts can also be wrapped with bacon strips or bacon and chicken livers, baked, and served as hot appetizers. They are excellent skewered with mushrooms, shrimp, tomatoes, and bell peppers and lightly barbecued.

Experiment. Artichokes—both fresh and marinated—are very adaptable.

The artichoke, like so many other foods, was believed to be an aphrodisiac. The early Greeks recommended that mothers desiring to bear a male child eat them in copious quantities.

SALADS
&
COLD DISHES

Artichokes, fresh or processed, add elegance and pizazz to what would otherwise be an everyday salad. Add coarsely chopped or sliced marinated artichoke hearts to a favorite cole slaw, macaroni, or potato salad recipe. The marinade can be mixed with the dressing to give the salad a little extra flavor.

Artichoke hearts are also very good added to bean salads. Instead of using a sweet dressing, use a vinaigrette dressing and add the artichoke hearts and their marinade.

Leftover artichokes, either marinated or not, can be stripped of their leaves and the bottoms chopped and added to salads, too. When a recipe for artichoke bottoms is used and there are leftover leaves, place them on a plate with a dish of homemade mayonnaise or other dipping sauce. It makes a quick and delicious salad in itself.

This is a summer favorite of mine, especially good when the sweet, big tomatoes are plentiful.

TOMATO-ARTICHOKE SALAD WITH BASIL

Using a plate or platter, depending on the number of people being served, line the dish with leaves of butter, red, or oak leaf lettuce or escarole.

Slice red tomatoes into rounds and overlap them on the plate, making a circle.

In the center of the plate, place artichoke hearts or thinly sliced artichoke bottoms that have been marinated.

Finely chop fresh basil (about 1/2 cup for a dinner plate full of tomatoes and artichokes) and 2 scallions, and sprinkle over the tomatoes and artichokes.

Drizzle with vinaigrette dressing. Garnish with parsley or olives if desired.

This can be prepared up to two hours ahead and placed in the refrigerator. If the dish is slightly upturned, baste the salad a few times before serving.

ELEGANT GREEN SALAD WITH ARTICHOKE HEARTS

Butter lettuce or mixed greens (1/2 to 3/4 cup per person)
Spanish onions, thinly sliced
black olives, pitted or sliced
cherry tomatoes
marinated artichoke hearts
Feta cheese
toasted walnuts (1/2 cup for 4 servings)
1 tablespoon olive or walnut oil
vinaigrette dressing

Mix butter lettuce or mixed greens in a salad bowl. Add Spanish onion, broken into rings, black olives, cherry tomatoes, marinated artichoke hearts, and crumbled Feta cheese.

Toast walnuts lightly in the oven or in olive or walnut oil, on top of stove.

Add to salad just before serving.

Serve with a vinaigrette dressing made with olive or walnut oil and either a good wine vinegar or raspberry vinegar.

At the bearing of the flowre the Grasshoppers then doe loudest sing.

Herodotus on Artichokes

The following recipe has a somewhat expensive dressing as it calls for walnut oil and sherry vinegar. A simpler vinaigrette dressing can be substituted, though the flavor of walnut oil creates a unique and superb dressing.

ARTICHOKE SALAD WITH WALNUT VINAIGRETTE

6 to 12 artichoke bottoms
2 to 3 tablespoons lemon juice
6 radishes
2 large carrots
watercress or parsley garnish
FOR WALNUT VINAIGRETTE:
1/3 cup plus 1 tablespoon walnut oil
1-1/2 tablespoons beef broth
1 teaspoon lemon juice
1/3 cup plus 1 tablespoon safflower oil
1-1/2 tablespoons sherry vinegar
salt and pepper to taste

Prepare artichoke bottoms, then cook in 1 to 2 quarts water, with lemon juice, and salt to taste.

Drain artichokes and allow to cool.

When cool, slice into thin rounds (if using a food processor, use ultra thin slicing disc), and place in a mixing bowl. Pour *Walnut Vinaigrette* over artichokes and allow to chill at least 2 hours or up to 3 days.

To serve, drain bottoms, place on a bed of lettuce on a platter, overlapping the slices.

Finely shred or slice radishes and carrots. Place shredded carrots in clusters around artichokes and radishes in center.

Garnish with sprigs of watercress or parsley.

Pour vinaigrette over salad and serve.

WALNUT VINAIGRETTE:

Blend with whisk: walnut oil, beef broth, lemon juice, saffllower oil, sherry vinegar, and salt and pepper to taste.

This recipe is from Alice Waters' *Chez Panisse Menu Cookbook.*

ARTICHOKE & GRAPEFRUIT SALAD

6 large artichokes
juice and rinds of 1 lemon
4 handsful red lettuce hearts
3 ripe pink grapefruit
1 cup olive oil
1/4 cup raspberry vinegar (approx.)
salt and pepper to taste
chervil sprigs (optional)

Trim the leaves completely from the artichokes so that only the hearts remain. Remove the chokes, cut off stems, and pare the outside of the hearts to remove any green. Squeeze the juice of 1 lemon into a bowl, and add hearts, the lemon rinds, and cold water to cover.

Wash and dry red leaf lettuce hearts. Section pink grapefruit and remove all membranes and seeds.

Slice the artichoke hearts into 1/4-inch slices and cook them in boiling salted water with a little lemon juice for 1-1/2 to 2 minutes, until they are *al dente*. Drain them and refresh with cold water.

Marinate the hearts in 1/2 cup olive oil.

Make a vinaigrette with 1/2 cup olive oil, 1/4 cup raspberry vinegar, or to taste, and salt and pepper to taste.

Toss the lettuce in some of the vinaigrette and arrange it on salad plates. Alternate grapefruit sections with artichoke slices on top of the lettuce.

Drizzle the salads with more vinaigrette and a little of the olive oil from marinating the artichoke hearts. Garnish with chervil sprigs.

This quite unusual salad is also from Alice Water's *Chez Panisse Menu Cookbook*. The recipe calls for duck fat, but chicken fat or clarified butter could be substituted.

This salad can also be served cold by cooking the artichoke hearts ahead, and allowing them to marinate for several hours. Eliminate the hot fat. Toasted walnuts added just before serving makes a nice addition to this salad.

WARM SALAD OF CURLY ENDIVE & ARTICHOKES

6 artichokes
lemon juice or vinegar
1 pound curly endive
1/4 pound prosciutto
2 shallots
1/4 cup sherry vinegar
1 tablespoon Dijon style mustard (or more)
1/2 cup virgin olive oil
salt and pepper to taste
1/4 cup duck fat

Trim the leaves completely from artichokes so that only the hearts remain. Remove the chokes, cut off stems, and pare outside of the hearts to remove any remaining green. Slice hearts in 1/4-inch pieces and put in bowl with cold water and lemon juice or vinegar.

Trim and wash curly endive, using just the center leaves if the head is large. Dry the endive and break into small pieces. Thin-slice prosciutto.

Make the vinaigrette by dicing shallots and mixing them with sherry vinegar and Dijon style mustard. Whisk in virgin olive oil and season with more mustard if necessary and salt and pepper.

To assemble the salad, cook artichokes in boiling water with a little salt and lemon juice added. They should be cooked *al dente*, about 1-1/2 to 2 minutes.

Drain the artichokes and toss them, still hot, into some of the vinaigrette.

Toss the endive with some vinaigrette in a large salad bowl. Heat duck fat over low heat until it is very warm. Add the artichoke slices to the endive and drizzle fat over salad.

Toss and season with salt and pepper. Garnish with prosciutto.

This is a nice alternative to potato or macaroni salad and is especially nice served with lamb.

Begin soaking the bulgur at least 3 hours before serving. If possible, make the tabouli the night before or early in the morning. This gives the salad time to marinate. Bulgur wheat (also known as cracked wheat) can be purchased at most natural foods or specialty food stores.

TABOULI SALAD WITH ARTICHOKE HEARTS

1 cup bulgur wheat

1-1/2 cups boiling water or broth

1/4 cup lemon or lime juice (or more)

1 to 3 cloves garlic, pressed

1/2 cup scallions, chopped

2 teaspoons fresh mint (1/2 teaspoon dried), chopped or crumbled

1/4 cup olive oil or other salad oil

1 6-oz. jar marinated artichoke hearts

1/2 cup fresh parsley, chopped

salt and pepper to taste

1 cucumber

1 green pepper

1 cup garbanzo beans (optional)

olives

Feta cheese

hardboiled eggs for garnish

Put bulgur wheat in a large bowl. Pour boiling water or broth over wheat. Cover and let stand about 1/2 hour.

Add lemon and/or lime juice, garlic, scallions, mint, olive oil, marinade from marinated artichoke hearts, parsley, and salt and freshly ground pepper to taste.

Mix thoroughly and allow to marinate in refrigerator 2 to 3 hours.

Before serving add: artichoke hearts, coarsely chopped, cucumber, seeded and chopped, green pepper, seeded and chopped, and cooked garbanzo beans (optional). Adjust seasonings to taste.

I find that I often add more lemon juice as the wheat seems to absorb it quickly. Garnish with olives, Feta cheese, or hardboiled eggs.

The bottoms of raw artichokes are, in fact, good to eat, but they must be very fresh. They are often eaten raw in Europe. Here is a way to serve raw artichokes with either hot or cold sauces.

RAW ARTICHOKES WITH SAUCE

Allow 2 large raw artichokes for about 4 servings. Just before serving, break off all the green outer leaves down to the pale inner ones. With a knife, trim base and stem end, rubbing with a cut lemon or coating with vinegar to reduce discoloration.

To eat, break off leaves and dip into sauces. When base is exposed, trim out the choke and cut up the base to eat.

RECOMMENDED SAUCES: Any of the hot butter sauces, *Green Goddess*, *Aioli*, *Bagna Cauda* or *Remoulade* sauces.

Tony Leonardini, a Castroville artichoke grower, tells of a test pilot from the East Coast who was stationed near Castroville. The pilot was curious about the artichokes that Tony and his friend grew, so one day they gave him some especially nice artichokes to take home for dinner. When they next saw the pilot they asked how he had liked them. He looked at them strangely, then said, "You guys grow those things for a living?" They said, "Yeah." "And people buy them?" "Well sure," they replied. "Well," said the pilot, "those were the worst things I've ever eaten." Tony and his friend looked at each other, puzzled. Finally Tony said, "Well, how'd you cook them?" The pilot looked astonished. "You mean you have to cook them?"

Although commercially bottled marinated artichoke hearts are very good, the homemade version is superior in texture and quality. The following two recipes—both excellent—have some differences in ingredients and flavor. I recommend trying each recipe to choose a favorite.

ARTICHOKES VINAIGRETTE

6 large artichokes
6 tablespoons onion, chopped
6 tablespoons dry vermouth
6 tablespoons olive oil
salt and pepper to taste
1 cup dry wine
1/4 cup olive oil
2 cloves garlic, pressed

FOR VINAIGRETTE DRESSING:

1/3 cup red wine vinegar or lemon juice
2/3 cup salad oil
1 clove garlic, minced
1 tablespoon parsley, minced
1 tablespoon Dijon style mustard
salt and pepper to taste

Cook artichokes, trimmed, in boiling water for 5 minutes. Drain. Place artichokes in a roaster or other large pan so they stand upright.

Combine chopped onion, dry vermouth, olive oil, and salt and pepper to taste. Separate leaves of artichokes and fill with vermouth mixture.

Combine wine, olive oil, and pressed garlic. Pour into the bottom of the pan and cook over low heat 25 to 30 minutes.

Remove artichokes from broth and serve hot or cold with a vinaigrette sauce.

VINAIGRETTE SAUCE:

Combine red wine vinegar or lemon juice, salad oil, minced garlic, parsley, Dijon style mustard, and salt and pepper to taste, and blend thoroughly with whisk. This may be made in advance and stored in the refrigerator until ready to use.

ARTICHOKE HEARTS VINAIGRETTE

24 artichoke hearts (or 6 large artichokes)

2 bouillon cubes (or 2 cups chicken stock)

1/2 cup dry vermouth (or white wine)

1/4 cup olive oil (or salad oil)

2 cloves garlic

1 teaspoon thyme leaves

1 bay leaf

1/8 teaspoon dry basil (or oregano)

2 tablespoons chives, chopped

6 hard-cooked eggs

10 to 12 cherry tomatoes

3 to 6 small celery spears

10 to 12 ripe olives

FOR VINAIGRETTE:

1/3 cup olive oil (or salad oil)

2 tablespoons white wine vinegar

1/2 teaspoon dry mustard

salt and pepper to taste

Combine artichoke hearts (or 6 large artichokes cut to bottoms then quartered), in a pot with 2 cups water and 2 bouillon cubes (or 2 cups chicken broth), dry vermouth, or white wine, olive oil (or salad oil), garlic, thyme, bay leaf, and dry basil (or oregano).

Bring to boil, cover and simmer until artichoke hearts are tender when pierced, about 20 minutes. Chill in cooking broth.

Lift artichokes from liquid and arrange on a serving platter or individual plates. Sprinkle with chives and accompany with hard-cooked eggs, cut in halves, cherry tomatoes, celery spears, and ripe olives.

Pour a vinaigrette sauce over artichokes.

VINAIGRETTE SAUCE: Blend olive oil (or salad oil), white wine vinegar, dry mustard, and salt and pepper to taste.

PICKLED ARTICHOKE HEARTS

small artichokes
1/2 cup vinegar per 2 to 3 cups water
cloves
cinnamon
whole black peppercorns
small chilis
garlic cloves
salt to taste
vinaigrette dressing

Prepare small artichokes as for hearts (or use frozen artichoke hearts).

Cook artichokes until just tender in water to which at least 1/2 cup vinegar has been added. You can also add to the water: cloves, cinnamon, whole black peppercorns, small chilis, and/or garlic cloves. Add salt to taste.

Let artichoke hearts cook in the liquid, then drain and serve, or marinate in a vinaigrette dressing.

This is a very pleasant recipe for a luncheon entrée but would also be nice for a light summer dinner.

CHILLED ARTICHOKE EGG SALAD

4 large artichokes, cooked and chilled
6 large eggs, cooked and chopped
1/3 cup celery, finely chopped
2 tablespoons green onion, sliced
1 3-1/4-oz. can tuna or albacore, drained and flaked
1/3 cup mayonnaise
1-1/2 teaspoons Dijon style mustard
fresh lemon juice
hot pepper sauce (optional)
salt and pepper to taste
parsley and paprika garnish

Remove center petals from artichokes.

In a mixing bowl, combine eggs, celery, green onion, and tuna or albacore.

Add mayonnaise, mustard, a dash of hot pepper sauce (optional), and lemon juice to taste.

Mix well, adjust seasonings to taste, and spoon into center of artichokes.

Garnish with paprika and fresh parsley.

In Italy artichokes are often eaten stems and all. This recipe is unusual in our country but is common in the outdoor cafes and trattorias of Rome. My adaptation of this unique recipe includes the stems, but if you can only find stemmed artichokes, use them. They will be delicious as they are.

ROMAN ARTICHOKE PLATTER

medium artichokes, 1 to 2 per person
vinaigrette dressing (about 1 cup for 10 to 12 artichokes)
butter or other lettuce leaves
cherry tomatoes
scallions
black olives
Italian salami slices
Provolone cheese slices

Break off outer leaves of artichokes down to the pale inner green ones. With a knife, slice off about the top third of leaves, then peel green surface from base and stem. Trim stem end.

Cook until tender, drain well, and lay out gently in a shallow dish. Pour vinaigrette dressing over artichokes.

Cover lightly and let stand until they reach room temperature, turning occasionally in dressing.

Cover the bottom of a platter with lettuce leaves. Stand the artichokes on the leaves and drizzle dressing over them. Garnish the platter with cherry tomatoes, scallions, black olives, and slices of Italian salami and Provolone cheese.

Serve at room temperature.

This recipe is adapted from *The Seasonal Kitchen* by Perla Meyers. It is an excellent recipe to use leftover poached or baked salmon, or purchase a small piece of salmon and prepare it by poaching in wine. This recipe is somewhat time consuming and expensive, but very much worth it for a special dinner party where it would make an excellent first course.

ARTICHOKE BOTTOMS WITH SALMON MOUSSE

6 very large artichokes or 12 medium artichokes

1 tablespoon lemon juice

2 tablespoons flour

2 cups flaked poached salmon

3 tablespoons mayonnaise

1 tablespoon fresh dill, finely minced (or 1/2 teaspoon dried dill)

salt and pepper to taste

cayenne pepper (optional)

up to 3 tablespoons whipped cream

paprika, capers, dill, and olives for garnish

FOR LEMON VINAIGRETTE:

juice of 1 lemon

1 teaspoon Dijon style mustard

1 teaspoon granulated sugar

6 tablespoons olive oil

2 tablespoons green onion or chives, minced

salt and pepper

Cut the stems off the artichokes and remove the first few layers of outer leaves. When the leaves become light green and bend forward, cut them off with a sharp knife close to the base. Rub the cut parts immediately with the cut side of 1/2 lemon.

In a large saucepan combine flour, lemon juice, and water. Bring the mixture to a boil, add a pinch of salt and the artichoke bottoms, and cook for 20 to 30 minutes or just until tender. Do not overcook.

Cool and dry well on paper towels. As soon as they are cool enough to handle, remove the choke with a grapefruit spoon and trim the artichoke bottoms with a sharp knife.

Make the lemon vinaigrette and pour over the artichoke bottoms. Cover the bowl and let the bottoms marinate for 2 hours.

SALMON MOUSSE:

Puree salmon in a blender or food processor or chop very fine. Add mayonnaise, salt, white pepper, dill (or 1/2 teaspoon dried dill), and a touch of cayenne pepper (optional). Chill the mixture for 1 hour. If it seems too thick, thin it with up to 3 tablespoons whipped cream. The mixture should be thick.

Drain the artichoke bottoms, then top each one with a dome of salmon mousse. Garnish by sprinkling each lightly with paprika. Make a little circle of capers on each dome and top with 2 tiny sprigs of dill and a black olive. Chill again and serve with buttered pumpernickel bread.

LEMON VINAIGRETTE:

In a small bowl, combine lemon juice, Dijon style mustard, sugar, olive oil, green onion or chives, and salt and pepper. Whisk until well blended and light.

ADDITIONAL SUGGESTIONS FOR COLD STUFFED ARTICHOKES

Fill cooked, chilled artichokes from which the center leaves and chokes have been removed with shrimp, crab meat or lobster salads prepared with mayonnaise, *Remoulade* or *Louis* dressings, chicken or duck salads with mayonnaise, or vegetable salad. Serve additional dressing on the side. Recipes for dressings can be found in the chapter on *Sauces*.

*Michael Boggiatto, general manager of
Delica-Sea in Castroville, tells of his grandfather
and partners who would sit in the packing sheds
at night, sorting the artichokes into bins,
separating them by size. Strong red wine,
usually made on the farm by the men, was
brought out and the workers told stories as they
sorted in the dim light. Several hours and bottles
of wine later, all the artichokes began looking the
same size. In the morning they often had to sort
the bins again.*

SOUPS

Down the coast from San Francisco the sleepy little town of Pescadero sits nestled between the ocean and the gentle slopes of the hills leading to the Santa Cruz mountains. For many years Pescadero was a thriving community. Around the turn of the century it was a fishing village, a farm town, and a resort. In 1895 Frank Duarte ran a saloon with hotel rooms upstairs—50¢ for rooms with a coastside view, 25¢ for a room in the back. In 1936 son Frank and his wife Emma converted the saloon into a bar and restaurant. The family had their own fishing boat, the back acres provided berries, artichokes, and other fresh produce, and Emma was famous for her delectable pies. This delightful little restaurant, run now by Frank and Emma's son, Ron, is still offering fresh seafood, cioppino, homemade pies, and artichoke specialties, especially omelettes, salads, and soup.

It is well worth a visit to Duarte's for a bowl of their famous hot artichoke soup and sourdough french bread. But if geography presents a problem, this specialty can be made at home.

RON & LYNN DUARTE'S ARTICHOKE SOUP

1 dozen small artichokes
salad oil
salt, pepper and garlic
to taste
small amount chicken
broth
large pat of butter
1/2 to 1 pint heavy cream
3 tablespoons cornstarch
if necessary

Cook the small artichokes in water, adding a little salad oil, salt, pepper, and garlic to the water. Cook until they are *al dente*. (The whole artichoke can be cooked, or it can be cut down to the heart before cooking.)

Drain artichokes in a pan until cool enough to handle. Cut artichoke hearts into quarters and place in a blender with enough chicken broth to make a puree.

When all artichoke hearts are blended, pour into a pan and add large pat of butter and sweet cream until the desired thickness is reached. If the soup is too thin, mix cornstarch with 1/2 cup cream, and add to warm soup.

Cook on medium heat until thickened.

Serves 4 to 6.

A similar soup but with more exacting proportions.

CREAM OF ARTICHOKE SOUP

4 large or medium
artichokes
1/2 cup celery, finely
chopped
1/2 cup onion, finely
chopped
6 tablespoons butter
6 tablespoons flour
6 cups chicken broth
1/4 cup lemon juice
1 bay leaf
1/4 teaspoon thyme
1/4 teaspoon nutmeg
salt and pepper to taste
1-3/4 cup milk
1/4 cup sour cream
2 egg yolks, beaten

Cook artichokes until tender. Drain and cool. Remove chokes and scrape meat from leaves. Chop hearts.

Sauté celery and onion in butter. Add flour. Cook 1 minute, stirring constantly, then blend in chicken broth and lemon juice. Add bay leaf, thyme, and nutmeg (optional), and salt and pepper to taste. Add artichoke hearts and scrapings.

Cover and simmer 20 minutes, then puree in a blender.

Mix together milk, sour cream, and egg yolks, beaten. If serving the soup cold, stir in milk mixture with a whisk, correct seasonings, and chill. If serving hot, heat the soup to the boiling point, remove from heat, and add milk mixture with a whisk. Season to taste, and keep warm on very low heat.

Serves 8.

VARIATIONS:

This soup can be made without cream or milk; simply use more chicken broth and bring to the desired thickness. Save one or two artichoke hearts to chop finely and add to soup, or use sautéed mushroom pieces or thinly sliced scallions and a thin slice of lemon to decorate soup. To make a vegetarian soup, cook the artichokes in vegetable stock or half wine and half water, covering the artichokes only half way to cook. Reduce this stock and use in place of chicken broth. A very light miso based soup can also be used instead of chicken broth.

This is a Cajun recipe from Louisiana where oysters are incorporated in many meals. Artichokes and oysters are well matched. This soup is especially good made one day ahead, allowing the flavors to blend well.

OYSTER & ARTICHOKE SOUP

4 large artichokes
1/2 cup butter
1/2 cup green onions, finely chopped
1 outer rib celery with leaves, finely chopped
1 medium carrot, chopped or grated
1 tablespoon fresh parsley, finely chopped
2 cloves garlic, pressed
1/2 teaspoon thyme
1 bay leaf
3 tablespoons flour
1 quart chicken stock
1/4 teaspoon anise seeds
1/4 teaspoon cayenne pepper
1 teaspoon Worcestershire sauce
1 quart oysters, chopped
1/2 cup vermouth
1/4 cup white wine
1/4 cup light cream
1 teaspoon lemon juice
grated rind of 1 lemon
salt to taste

Warm chicken stock on low heat.

Cook artichokes. Scrape artichoke leaves, chop hearts, and reserve.

In a 4 quart heavy pot, melt butter and sauté chopped green onions, rib celery, carrot, chopped parsley, garlic, thyme, and bay leaf, until celery and carrot are tender.

Add artichoke scrapings and hearts. Stir well.

Slowly stir in flour, but do not brown. Add the warmed chicken stock, a little at a time, anise seeds, cayenne pepper, Worcestershire sauce, and salt to taste.

Simmer 15 minutes.

Add chopped oysters, drained (reserving liquid).

Cook over low heat 10 minutes. Add vermouth, white wine, light cream, lemon juice and the grated lemon rind, and oyster liquid. Remove bay leaf. Blend until smooth.

Heat and serve.

Hugo Tottino's father came from Italy as a young man, sponsored by his adoptive father who paid his way, telling him to pay back the money after he had made several thousand dollars. The elder Tottino fully intended to return to Italy, but ended up sending the money back after becoming one of the pioneer Castroville artichoke farmers. Hugo was born shortly after his father began farming in Castroville. By the time he was eight he was building artichoke boxes and helping to hand-dig the irrigation trenches. His labor paid off in the long run. Hugo has been an extremely influential person in making the California artichoke industry what it is today. Hugo also loves to eat, and fortunately married a superb cook. This is Dolores Tottino's version of sauteed artichokes.

DOLORES TOTTINO'S ARTICHOKE SOUP

3-1/4 cups beef broth
6 artichoke bottoms and stems, peeled and cooked
2 tablespoons onion, chopped
1/4 cup carrots, shredded
1/4 cup potatoes, shredded
2 tablespoons butter (or margarine)
salt and pepper
smoked ham, chopped (optional)

Put 3 cups of beef broth in a pot with the chopped onion, carrots, and potatoes. Simmer 15 minutes.

While the broth and vegetables cook, put through ricer or food processor 5 artichoke bottoms and the peeled and cooked stems. Add to broth.

Chop 1 artichoke bottom and add to broth.

Melt butter (or margarine) and add flour. Gradually add 1/4 cup beef broth, stirring well, until blended and thickened. Add to soup, blend, and add salt and pepper to taste.

Bring to a boil and serve. If desired, chopped smoked ham can be added.

ARTICHOKE SOUP

1 6-oz. jar marinated
artichoke hearts
1/4 cup onion, chopped
1 cup celery, sliced
1 cube chicken bouillon
(or 1/2 cup chicken stock)
2 teaspoons cornstarch
2 cups half and half
1 tablespoon lemon juice
salt and peppr
croutons (optional)

Drain marinade from jar of marinated artichoke hearts and cut larger ones in half. Spoon off 2 tablespoons of the marinade and put the balance in a saucepan.

Add chopped onion and sliced celery and sauté until tender-crisp. Add 1/2 cup water and 1 cube chicken bouillon (or 1/2 cup chicken stock). Cover and simmer 10 minutes.

Stir cornstarch into half and half and add to hot mixture.

Cook, stirring, until mixture boils and thickens slightly.

Add artichokes to soup and stir in lemon juice. Season to taste with salt and pepper and garnish with croutons.

Another quick artichoke soup—a good recipe to use up any leftover artichokes.

ARTICHOKE & SHRIMP SOUP

2 tablespoons butter or
margarine
1/4 cup green onions, finely
chopped
1/4 teaspoon dried thyme
2 10-1/2-oz. cans
condensed tomato soup
1 cup cooked artichoke
hearts or bottoms
1 cup cooked shrimp
1/2 cup cooked rice
2 teaspoons lemon juice
salt and pepper to taste

Heat butter or margarine in a large saucepan. Add green onions and thyme and cook about 4 minutes, stirring occasionally.

Add condensed tomato soup and 2 cans water, stirring until blended. Add artichoke hearts or bottoms, shrimp, and cooked rice.

Season to taste with salt and pepper and heat thoroughly.

Remove from heat and add lemon juice. Serve hot.

A local grower picked some fresh artichokes for a dinner party for some friends visiting on vacation. That evening as he began to prepare the artichokes one of the visitors said, "Gee, I didn't know you could just go ahead and cook them. I thought you had to let them ripen first."

ENTRÉES

James Beard, in *American Cookery,* said about artichokes: "There is no printed record of artichokes in America, nor directions for cooking them, before about the last third of the nineteenth century. Curiously enough, they were called French artichokes at that time, and no credit was given to the Italians, who must have imported some of the globes as well . . .

"Mrs. Rorer, in her 1885 edition, described them as having a head like a pinecone and advised serving them with Hollandaise. Miss Farmer, in the 1896 and 1904 editions, noted that most artichokes were imported from France, but went on to say that there were those which arrived from California later in the year."

The following two recipes are from *American Cookery*. Of the first recipe, Beard said: "This recipe, of French-Italian origin, is thoroughly different and exceedingly good."

BAKED STUFFED ARTICHOKES

4 large artichokes
1 clove garlic, finely chopped
6 tablespoons olive oil
1/2 cup mushrooms, chopped
1/2 cup ham, chopped
1 cup dry breadcrumbs
1/2 teaspoon salt
1/2 teaspoon freshly ground pepper
1/4 teaspoon thyme
1/4 teaspoon oregano
olive oil
broth or white wine
Parmesan cheese, grated

Preheat oven to 375 degrees.

Cut the tops from artichokes, remove the stalks, and cook the artichokes in boiling, salted, acidulated water until done.

While they are cooking, sauté garlic in olive oil a few minutes, then add mushrooms, ham, breadcrumbs, salt, pepper, thyme, and oregano. Toss lightly but well.

When the artichokes are cooked, remove the chokes and center leaves and spread the surrounding leaves back to provide a well for the filling. Fill with some of the mushroom-ham mixture and also spoon the mixture between the leaves. Tie the artichokes securely around the middle.

Sprinkle well with olive oil, place in a baking dish, and add about 1 inch broth or white wine.

Bake 30 minutes, basting twice with pan juices. Five minutes before finishing, sprinkle a spoonful of Parmesan cheese on each one. Untie and serve as a main course at luncheon or as a first or side course at dinner.

Mr. Beard recorded this recipe from *The Neighborhood Cookbook*, published in 1914. This is an interesting and unusual way to use sweetbreads.

MRS. FLEISCHNER'S STUFFED ARTICHOKES

6 large artichokes
2 slices bread
1/4 cup heavy cream
1/4 cup sherry
1 pair blanched sweetbreads, finely diced and sauteed in butter
butter for sautéing
bouillon or stock
6 mushroom caps, sauteed

Preheat oven to 350 degrees.

Cut about 1-1/2 inches from the tops of the artichokes and discard. Trim the bottoms so that artichokes will stand easily.

Cook until tender. Remove from water and drain. Let cool.

While cooling cooked artichokes, soak bread in milk, then squeeze dry and break into little bits. Set aside.

When artichokes are cool enough to handle, extract the centers and chokes, preparing for stuffing. Scrape off edible pulp from center leaves. Chop or puree the pulp for use below.

Combine pulp with bread bits, heavy cream, and sherry. Beat together lightly, and combine with sweetbreads.

In heavy pan heat all together over low heat. Adjust seasonings to taste.

When warmed through and well blended, spoon into artichokes. Place in baking dish a little bouillon or stock. Cover lightly with foil or paper and bake 25 to 30 minutes until piping hot.

Top each artichoke with sautéed mushroom cap.

The following two recipes involve stuffing artichokes with chicken. The first recipe calls for the artichokes to be cut in half, and curry and almonds are the distinctive flavors. The second recipe uses the more traditional sherry and tarragon as flavors.

CHICKEN STUFFED ARTICHOKES

6 fresh artichokes
1 teaspoon salt
1/4 cup butter
2 green onions, chopped
1/4 cup flour
1 teaspoon curry powder
1 cup half and half (or light cream)
1 cup cooked chicken, chopped
1/2 cup mushrooms, chopped
2 tablespoons dry white wine
1/4 cup breadcrumbs
1/4 cup blanched almonds

Cut artichokes in half crosswise. Discard top half. Trim about 1/2 inch off tip of each leaf. Cut stem off at base.

Pour water 2 to 3 inches deep in a 4 to 5 quart pot. Add 1 teaspoon salt. Bring water to boil.

Carefully add artichoke halves, 1 at a time. Cover and simmer 20 minutes or until tender.

Remove artichokes. Drain, upside down on paper towels.

Preheat oven to 350 degrees. With a spoon, scoop out chokes.

In a medium saucepan melt butter. Add onions and sauté 2 to 3 minutes. Stir in flour, curry, and salt and pepper to taste.

Add green onions, and saute 2 to 3 minutes.

Pour in half and half. Cook, stirring constantly, until thickened.

Stir in chicken, mushrooms, and white wine. Spoon into drained artichoke halves.

In a small bowl combine breadcrumbs and blanched almonds. Sprinkle over stuffed artichokes.

Bake 20 to 30 minutes or until tops are golden. Serve hot.

CHICKEN & TARRAGON STUFFED ARTICHOKES

4 to 5 large artichokes
1/4 cup butter
3 tablespoons flour
1 cup chicken broth
1 cup light cream
2 tablespoons sherry
1/2 teaspoon tarragon
2 cups chicken, diced
salt and pepper to taste

Preheat oven to 350 degrees.

Cook artichokes until tender. Drain and cool. Prepare artichokes for stuffing. Set in baking dish.

Melt butter and blend in flour. Slowly stir in chicken broth, light cream, and sherry and cook until mixture thickens.

Mix in tarragon, diced chicken, and salt and pepper to taste.

Stuff artichokes with chicken mixture and heat thoroughly, about 10 to 15 minutes.

Joe Carcione, California's "Green Grocer," has a fine reputation both for his information on selecting fresh produce as well as preparing it for optimal flavor. This is his recipe for stuffed artichokes which is a very traditional Italian style.

JOE CARCIONE'S STUFFED ARTICHOKES

4 large artichokes
olive oil
FOR FILLING:
1-1/2 cups breadcrumbs
1/2 cup Romano or Parmesan cheese, grated
olive oil
1 clove garlic, minced
3 tablespoons parsley, chopped
salt and pepper to taste

Mix the filling all together, using a little of the olive oil to moisten the breadcrumbs. Set aside.

Remove small leaves at bottom of artichokes. Cut off stems and clip each leaf with scissors.

Stuff filling between leaves of artichokes, working from the outside to the center until leaves are too tightly together to be filled.

In a heavy pot with about 1/2-inch of water in bottom, place artichokes so they touch. Pour a little olive oil over each artichoke to hold stuffing firm and moist.

Bring water to boil, then reduce to simmer and put cover on pot. Simmer about 1 hour or until leaves are easy to pull away from artichokes.

Sotere Torregian, a scholar, poet, teacher and librarian, provided helpful and colorful information for this book. Most recently from Lebanon, the Torregian family came to the United States, bringing with them a rich heritage of recipes. Of his family's method of preparing artichokes, Sotere says: "The origin of this particular recipe goes beyond Lebanon, probably back to Palestine of the Pre-Christian era, and was brought to Sicily by our Arab ancestors."

A real similarity exists between Joe Carcione's recipe and this one of Sotere's, perhaps demonstrating how the preparation of many foods is passed on from one area to the next, with adaptations made by each new group of people.

SOTERE TORREGIAN'S STUFFED ARTICHOKES

1/4 cup olive oil
1/2 to 2/3 cup Kasseri cheese, grated
1 1/2 cups breadcrumbs
1 to 3 cloves garlic, minced or pressed
4 to 6 artichokes
olive oil
salt and pepper to taste

Prepare the artichokes in the same manner as for Joe Carcione's recipe. Fill pot with a few inches of water.

Mix together olive oil, Kasseri cheese (Kasseri is a hard Greek cheese that can be purchased in many cheese shops or specialty food stores), breadcrumbs, garlic, and salt to taste.

Stuff mixture between the leaves of artichokes, pour a little olive oil on each, and cook until tender, about 1 hour.

Dip artichoke petals into olive oil and garlic. Serve with warm pita bread.

A third stuffed artichoke recipe that is similar to the two above comes from Michelle Schmidt's *New Almond Cookery*. The toasted almonds add pleasantly crunchy texture and delicate flavor.

STUFFED ARTICHOKES

4 medium artichokes
2 tablespoons lemon juice
3/4 cup whole almonds, toasted
3/4 cup fresh white breadcrumbs
3/4 cup Parmesan cheese, grated
1/2 cup parsley, chopped
1/4 cup butter, softened
2 tablespoons shallots, chopped
1 teaspoon lemon peel, grated
2 cloves garlic, chopped finely
9 tablespoons olive oil
salt and pepper

Preheat oven to 350 degrees.

Trim the stems from artichokes, remove tough outer leaves, and slice 1/3 off the top of each artichoke. Gently spread the leaves apart and remove the choke from the center.

Place artichokes in 1 quart water to which 1 tablespoon lemon juice has been added.

In food processor or blender, coarsely chop almonds. Combine with breadcrumbs, Parmesan cheese, parsley, butter, shallots, lemon peel, garlic, and 4 tablespoons olive oil.

Drain artichokes. Divide stuffing equally among artichokes, filling the centers and pressing stuffing among the leaves.

Pour 1/2 cup water into a shallow, earthenware baking dish. Arrange artichokes in dish.

Combine 5 tablespoons olive oil and 1 tablespoon lemon juice and drizzle over artichokes. Season with salt and pepper. Bake 1 hour or until artichoke hearts are tender when pierced with a knife.

ARTICHOKES WITH SEAFOOD

8 large artichokes
1/4 cup butter
8 green onions, chopped
2 garlic cloves, pressed
1 pound mushrooms, sliced
2 pounds scallops or shrimp (or 2 pounds firm fleshed fish)
1-1/2 cups croutons
1 tablespoon fresh tarragon (or 1 teaspoon dried tarragon)
1 teaspoon fresh dill (or 1/2 teaspoon dried)
1/2 teaspoon celery seed
1/2 teaspoon paprika
1/4 cup dry sherry
1-1/2 cups Hollandaise sauce

Cook artichokes, remove center leaves and chokes, and prepare for stuffing.

Melt butter in 10 to 12-inch skillet. Add green onions, garlic, and mushrooms. Sauté briefly over medium heat.

Add scallops or shrimp, cut in 1/2-inch pieces (or 2 pounds firm fleshed fish, shredded or chopped), croutons, tarragon, dill, celery seed, and paprika.

Heat, stirring constantly, just until seafood is cooked.

Add dry sherry and simmer 1 to 2 minutes. Season with salt and pepper.

Stir in *Hollandaise* sauce (see *Sauce* section).

Preheat oven to 350 degrees.

Spread artichoke leaves apart. Fill with seafood mixture, spooning any excess between leaves. Top artichokes with 1 cup *Hollandaise*.

Place on greased cookie sheet and tent with aluminum foil. Bake 10 to 15 minutes. Remove foil and place under broiler until tops are lightly browned.

Artichokes may be filled in advance and refrigerated. Bring to room temperature before baking.

A few years ago, Hank Sciaroni, San Francisco and San Mateo County Director and Farms Advisor; Vince Rubatsky, University of California Extension Service specialist; and Joe Gianinni, a long time artichoke grower, grew an experimental purple variety, *Magnifico*, on Joe's property in Pescadero.

It flourished on the coast and is considered by many to be superior both in quality and flavor to the *Green Globe*, but it didn't gain commercial popularity, even though in Italy purple artichokes are very common. The American public just wasn't ready for the purple version of an already curious food.

Scampi, a large shrimp from Italy and the Adriatic, has also not made a big showing in America, though the dish for which it is named is popular. Gulf or Alaska shrimp are usually substituted, and this dish is especially good with artichokes added.

ARTICHOKES & SHRIMP A LA SCAMPI

1 pound medium sized raw shrimp

12 egg sized artichoke hearts (or 4 large artichoke bottoms, quartered)

8 tablespoons butter

1 tablespoon green onions, minced

3 tablespoons olive oil

5 to 6 cloves garlic, minced

2 teaspoons lemon juice

salt to taste

1/4 cup white wine

3 tablespoons parsley, minced

1/2 teaspoon grated lemon peel

freshly ground pepper

Shell and devein the shrimp, rinse, and pat dry with paper towels. Set aside.

Pare artichoke hearts to the pale green leaves, cut in half, and remove chokes (or use quartered artichoke bottoms). Cook in acidulated water until just tender. Drain.

In a large frying pan melt butter. Stir in green onion, olive oil, garlic, lemon juice, and salt to taste. Cook until bubbly.

Add shrimp to pan and cook, stirring occasionally, until shrimp turn pink (about 4 to 5 minutes).

Add wine and artichoke hearts and cook until bubbly.

Add parsley, lemon peel, and pepper. Serve immediately.

If oysters are plentiful, this entrée casserole is well worth making. Two pounds fresh firm-fleshed fish could be substituted for the oysters.

OYSTER & ARTICHOKE CASSEROLE

6 to 8 artichokes (1 per person)
8 tablespoons butter
2-1/2 cups green onion, finely chopped
1/2 cup celery, finely chopped
1 10-oz. can cream of mushroom soup
1 tablespoon Worcestershire sauce
1/4 teaspoon Tabasco
1 tablespoon grated lemon rind
salt and pepper to taste
4 pints oysters
1/2 cup breadcrumbs
lemon slices and parsley as garnish

Preheat oven to 350 degrees.

Boil artichokes.

Scrape the leaves of artichokes. Mash scrapings with fork. Keep artichoke bottoms whole.

In a heavy skillet melt butter. Sauté green onion and celery.

Reduce heat and add cream of mushroom soup, Worcestershire sauce, Tabasco, lemon rind, and salt and pepper to taste. Simmer 10 minutes.

Add artichoke scrapings and oysters, drained on paper towels, and simmer 10 minutes. Arrange artichoke hearts on bottom of 2-quart casserole. Pour oyster mixture over hearts and top with breadcrumbs.

Bake 30 minutes. If necessary, spoon off excess liquid. Broil 3 to 5 minutes, or until breadcrumbs turn brown. Garnish with lemon slices and parsley.

This is a fast, easy recipe to assemble on short notice. Serve with plenty of hot french bread or over rice or pasta.

ANCHOVIED ARTICHOKES

2 tablespoons butter
3/4 cup sour cream
2 teaspoons anchovy paste
1/2 teaspoon salt
1/2 teaspoon pepper
1/2 teaspoon garlic salt
1/4 teaspoon Tabasco sauce
1/2 teaspoon paprika
2 teaspoons lemon juice
18 small artichokes (or 2 packages frozen artichoke hearts)

In a saucepan combine butter, sour cream, anchovy paste, salt, pepper, garlic salt, Tabasco sauce, paprika, and lemon juice. Cook over low heat 5 minutes, stirring occasionally.

While sauce is simmering, prepare small artichokes as for hearts and cook until tender (or cook the frozen artichoke hearts according to directions). Drain, cut in half, and add to saucepan.

Adjust seasonings and heat an additional 5 to 10 minutes.

The following four recipes can be prepared ahead, refrigerated, and baked until well heated when ready to serve. Shrimp, crab, firm-fleshed fish, or lobster or even a combination of two or more seafoods can be used in these dishes.

CRAB CASSEROLE WITH ARTICHOKE HEARTS

3 tablespoons flour
3 tablespoons butter
1 cup milk
1/2 cup medium sharp cheddar cheese, shredded
2 teaspoons Worcestershire sauce
18 to 24 small artichokes (or 2 packages frozen artichoke hearts)
2 cups crabmeat, shredded
Parmesan cheese
1/4 cup fresh parsley, chopped

Preheat oven to 300 degrees.

In saucepan melt butter.

Mix in flour, and gradually stir in milk. Cook until thickened, stirring constantly.

Blend in cheddar cheese and Worcestershire sauce. Cook until cheese melts.

Cook the small artichokes and prepare as for hearts (or prepare the frozen artichoke hearts according to directions). Drain.

Spoon 1/4 of sauce into bottom of casserole dish. Alternate layers of cooked and drained artichoke hearts and crabmeat (save some for garnish), putting 1/2 of sauce between layers.

Cover top with remaining sauce and sprinkle with Parmesan cheese.

Bake 30 minutes.

When serving, garnish casserole with remaining artichoke hearts and crabmeat and parsley.

SHRIMP & ARTICHOKE CASSEROLE

8 to 10 artichoke hearts
1-1/2 pounds shrimp
1/2 pound fresh mushrooms
1/2 cup butter
1/4 cup flour
1 cup heavy cream
1/2 cup milk
1/4 cup dry sherry
1 tablespoon Worcestershire sauce
salt and pepper to taste
1/4 cup fresh Parmesan cheese
1/4 teaspoon paprika

Preheat oven to 300 degrees.

In bottom of well greased 1-1/2 quart casserole, place artichoke hearts and shrimp.

Sauté mushrooms in 1/4 cup butter until soft and tender. Pour over shrimp.

Melt another 1/4 cup butter and add flour, cooking over low heat 3 to 5 minutes, stirring constantly.

Gradually add heavy cream and milk, cooking until thick.

Add dry sherry, Worcestershire sauce, and salt and pepper to taste. Stir until smooth. Pour over casserole.

Top with freshly grated Parmesan cheese and paprika and bake 25 minutes until lightly brown and bubbly.

ARTICHOKE HALVES WITH CRAB

5 to 6 medium artichokes
1 tablespoon butter
1-1/2 tablespoons flour
2/3 cup chicken broth
1/2 cup light cream or milk
1/2 teaspoon basil
1 pound crabmeat
3/4 cup Swiss cheese,
shredded

Preheat oven to 400 degrees.

Trim artichokes down to inner green leaves and cut green surface from base and stems. Cut in halves lengthwise.

Cook until tender, drain well, and scoop out choke.

While artichokes are cooking, melt butter and blend with flour. Gradually add chicken broth, light cream or milk, and basil. Cook, stirring, until boiling and slightly thickened.

Remove from heat and mix in crabmeat.

Pour crab into a 1 to 1-1/2-quart shallow casserole. On top, arrange side by side the cooked artichoke halves, cupped side up. Sprinkle with Swiss cheese, covering artichokes well to prevent drying.

Bake uncovered about 12 minutes or until sauce is bubbling. (To make dish ahead, assemble, cover and chill; uncover and bake for about 20 minutes or until bubbling).

Makes 4 to 5 servings.

ARTICHOKE BOTTOMS STUFFED WITH CRAB

8 artichoke bottoms
1/2 cup scallions, chopped
1/2 pound mushrooms
2 cloves garlic, pressed
3/4 cup butter
1/2 pound fresh crabmeat
1/2 cup flour
2 cups fish stock or
chicken broth
2 cups cream
salt and pepper to taste
lemon wedges and parsley
as garnish

Prepare artichoke bottoms. Set cupped side up on a warm platter or plate.

While artichokes are cooking, sauté scallions, mushrooms, and garlic in 1/4 cup butter for about 2 minutes.

Add crabmeat and cook just until crab is warm.

In another pan melt 1/2 cup butter. Stir in flour. Add fish stock (or chicken broth) and cream slowly, stirring until thickened. Season to taste.

Spoon crab mixture into artichoke bottoms and top with sauce. Sprinkle with paprika and garnish with lemon wedges and parsley.

This is a unique version of Coquilles St. Jacques, *very* good. A thick sour cream or cream can be substituted for the *Creme Fraiche* if necessary.

VELOUTE DE COQUILLES ST. JACQUES ET ARTICHAUTS

24 large bay scallops
salt and pepper
2 tablespoons butter
3 tablespoons shallots, finely chopped
3 medium artichoke bottoms, cooked and diced
1/3 cup dry white wine
1 tablespoon cognac
2 cups fish stock
2 cups creme fraiche (or 2 cups thick sour cream)
FOR CREME FRAICHE:
2 cups cream
4 tablespoons buttermilk

Sprinkle scallops with salt and pepper.

In large saucepan melt butter. Add shallots and sauté until tender, about 3 minutes (do not let turn brown).

Add scallops, artichoke bottoms, and wine. Cook until just done, about 2 minutes.

Remove from heat and transfer scallops and artichokes to another pan using a slotted spoon. Sprinkle with cognac and keep warm.

Add fish stock to cooking liquid. Place over high heat and boil, skimming foam from surface as necessary until liquid is reduced to 1/2 cup, about 30 minutes.

Blend in 2 cups *Creme Fraiche*. Return to boil, then reduce heat and simmer 1 minute.

Pour through a fine strainer into scallop-artichoke mixture. Warm until just heated through. Taste and adjust seasonings and serve immediately.

CREME FRAICHE:

In a large jar with a tight fitting lid combine cream and buttermilk. Shake well. Let stand in a warm, draft-free area for at least 12 hours (depending on the warmth of the area it might take 24 to 36 hours before it has thickened) before using. *Creme Fraiche* can be made ahead and kept in the refrigerator for 2 to 3 weeks. Makes 1 cup *Creme Fraiche*.

ARTICHOKE BOTTOMS EN SOUFFLE

6 large artichoke bottoms (or 12 small artichoke bottoms)
2 tablespoons sweet butter
5 tablespoons butter
2 shallots, finely chopped
1 cup fresh crabmeat, finely minced
2 teaspoons lemon juice
salt and pepper
1 cup milk
couple sprigs thyme, parsley
3 tablespoons flour
4 egg yolks
1/2 teaspoon dry mustard
1/2 cup Gruyere, finely grated (or fresh Parmesan cheese or mixture of both)

Preheat oven to 375 degrees.

Poach artichoke bottoms until *al dente*, then sauté in sweet butter. Place in a large baking dish.

In a small skillet melt 2 tablespoons butter. Add minced shallots and cook until they are soft, but not browned.

Add crabmeat and lemon juice. Season with salt and pepper and cook over very low heat until mixture is heated through. Reserve.

Heat milk with a couple of sprigs each of fresh thyme and parsley, and simmer for 10 minutes. Remove from heat and remove thyme and parsley.

In a heavy-bottomed saucepan melt 3 tablespoons butter. Add flour and cook for 2 minutes, stirring constantly, without letting it brown. Add the hot milk all at once and keep stirring until the mixture gets very thick and smooth.

Remove the saucepan from heat and add egg yolks, one at a time, incorporating each yolk completely into the sauce before adding the next one.

Season the mixture with salt, pepper, and dry mustard.

Return the saucepan to the heat and whisk sauce until well heated. Do not boil.

Remove from heat and fold in crabmeat mixture. Add Gruyere or fresh Parmesan cheese, or a mixture of both.

In 1983 Michael Jackson and Horace Mercurio opened the Moss Landing Oyster Bar and Company, a delightful restaurant tucked between Moss Landing on the water, and Castroville, slightly inland. Specialties are the abundant seafoods from Central and Northern California, but Michael and Horace have also incorporated the use of local produce and wine in their establishment. Artichokes, strawberries, lettuce, and other produce in season come exclusively from Monterey County, as do the fine wines they serve.

They often serve *Eggs Neptune* as the specialty. This recipe makes Eggs Benedict pale by comparison.

EGGS NEPTUNE

FOR 1 TO 2 SERVINGS:
3 oz. butter
2 tablespoons shallots
4 oz. crabmeat
1/4 cup mushrooms, sliced
1 teaspoon paprika
salt and pepper
1/4 cup artichoke hearts, cooked and quartered
1 cup heavy cream
English muffin
2 poached eggs
Bernaise sauce (See Sauce section)
parsley and chopped black olives as garnish

In a hot pan add butter and shallots and simmer 1 minute.

Add crabmeat, mushrooms, paprika, and salt and pepper to taste. Cook until soft.

Add artichoke hearts and heavy cream. Cook until sauce is reduced by half.

Pour mixture over a split and toasted English muffin. Top each half with a poached egg and cover with *Bernaise* sauce.

Garnish with chopped parsley and chopped black olives.

Another of Michael Jackson's marvelous artichoke recipes, this one is a lovely first course for an elegant dinner. It also is ideal for the entrée for a romantic dinner for two.

ARTICHOKES PROVENCALE

*1 tablespoon shallots
(or green onions),
finely chopped*

*1 tablespoon garlic, finely
minced*

2 oz. clarified butter

1/2 cup tomato, diced

1/4 cup mushrooms, sliced

1/8 cup green onions, sliced

*16 to 20 prawns, peeled
and deveined*

1 cube butter

salt and pepper

1 large artichoke

*chopped parsley and
scallions as garnish*

Sauté shallots (or scallions) and garlic in clarified butter.

Add diced tomato, mushrooms, and onions. Cook until nearly soft, adding 16 to 20 prawns for the last 3 to 4 minutes of sautéing.

Add salt and freshly ground pepper to taste and cube butter. Allow the ingredients to sit while preparing artichoke, so that flavors can meld.

Cook artichoke, then cut in half and clean out inner choke and small green leaves. Fan the artichoke leaves out on a plate. Fill the center depression with prawns, then pour the sauce over prawns and artichoke halves.

Garnish with chopped parsley and onions.

The Boggiattos tell of Antonio and Gussie Boggiatto who started farming artichokes in 1925. In 1929 Antonio decided to pull out the small plot of artichokes on their 100 acre ranch to put in cauliflower and lettuce which had been enormously successful on the market the year before. Gussie talked her husband into letting her tend the artichokes rather than pulling them out. The market collapsed for lettuce and cauliflower that year, but the artichokes saved the ranch, and the Boggiattos have stuck with artichokes ever since. Additionally, they now own and operate the major packing house for the farmers from Half Moon Bay to Santa Cruz.

Albina Boggiatto, Gussie's daughter-in-law, has passed on this family recipe, a favorite for many years. She suggests that it be served as a side dish for roasts.

GUSSIE BOGGIATTO'S SAUTÉED ARTICHOKES

8 small artichokes
2 tablespoons olive oil
2 tablespoons butter
3 cloves garlic, minced
1/4 cup fresh parsley, chopped
1/2 teaspoon dried basil
2 teaspoons dried oregano
1/2 teaspoon dried rosemary
salt and pepper to taste
1/2 cup white wine or chicken stock

Clean, trim, and halve or quarter artichokes. Hold in acidulated water.

In a medium skillet heat olive oil and butter.

Add drained artichokes and garlic and brown slightly, stirring to coat all sides.

Stir in parsley, basil, oregano, rosemary, salt and pepper to taste, and white wine or chicken stock.

Cover and steam over low heat until artichokes are tender, about 20 minutes. If too much liquid remains, uncover and cook over higher heat until slightly crisp.

Serves 4.

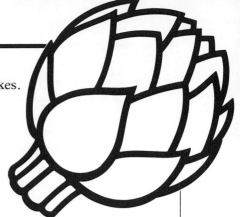

Joy Pieri offers her family version of sautéed artichokes.

JOY PIERI'S SIMPLY DELICIOUS ARTICHOKE SAUTÉ

1/4 cup olive oil
10 to 12 baby artichokes, trimmed and quartered
2 garlic cloves
1/4 cup fresh parsley, chopped
1 teaspoon Italian herb mix
salt and pepper to taste
1 cup white wine

In a large skillet heat olive oil.

Add baby artichokes and sauté briefly on all sides.

Stir in garlic cloves, parsley, Italian herb mixture, salt and pepper to taste, and wine. Cover and simmer until artichokes are tender but still crunchy, about 15 to 20 minutes.

May be prepared ahead and reheated to serve.

ARTICHOKE SAUTÉ WITH MUSTARD & CHIVES

2/3 cup natural almonds, chopped
1 tablespoon oil
24 tiny fresh artichokes (or 2 packages frozen artichoke hearts)
1/4 cup butter
2 tablespoons Dijon style mustard
1 tablespoon lemon juice
1/4 cup fresh parsley, chopped
2 tablespoons chives, finely chopped
2 tablespoons olive oil
salt and pepper to taste

Sauté almonds in oil until crisp. Reserve.

Prepare tiny artichokes as for artichoke hearts (or substitute 2 packages frozen artichoke hearts).

Plunge into boiling water for 3 to 4 minutes or just until tender. Drain. Thinly slice artichokes lengthwise. (If using frozen artichokes, thaw but don't boil.)

Sauté artichokes in butter 3 to 4 minutes. Add Dijon sytle mustard and lemon juice and sauté 1 minute longer.

Toss with almonds, parsley, chives, and olive oil. Season to taste with salt and pepper.

SAUTÉED ARTICHOKES

2 Italian sausages
1 small onion, chopped
1 to 2 cloves garlic, pressed
1/4 cup parsley, chopped
1/4 pound fresh mushrooms, sliced
10 to 12 small to medium artichoke hearts or bottoms, quartered
1/2 cup white wine
salt and pepper

Remove casings from Italian sausages and brown meat.

Add onion, garlic, parsley, artichokes, and mushrooms.

Add white wine and salt and pepper to taste. Cover and cook about 30 to 40 minutes on low heat, adding a little water if necessary.

This dish may be cooked in oven in covered casserole if preferred.

Hugo Tottino tells of being asked by a friend if he would send some artichokes to a couple in Michigan. He obliged by sending a box of the deluxe jumbo-sized artichokes. A few weeks later when he again saw his friend he asked how the Easterners had enjoyed the artichokes. "Well," the friend replied, "It seems they had never seen artichokes before, so they took them outside and planted them. Only problem was, they couldn't understand why they didn't start growing."

The following recipe is Valerie Phipps favorite artichoke dish. She exhibited it at the San Mateo County fair in 1983, serving samples and giving copies of the recipe to fair goers. I imagine she convinced everyone who tried the samples to immediately go home to prepare the dish for themselves.

VAL'S CHICKEN DELIGHT

1 large frying chicken, cut in pieces
3 tablespoons flour
2 tablespoons oil
2 cups chicken stock
1 cup whole mushrooms
2 cups artichoke hearts
1 tablespoon lemon juice
1 large clove garlic, pressed
1 teaspoon fresh oregano leaves (or 1/2 teaspoon dried oregano)
salt and pepper to taste

Dip chicken pieces in flour and brown in oil in a large skillet, then remove from pan.

Add the balance of flour to the hot fat left in the pan, stirring to loosen browned bits. Cook over medium heat until golden brown.

Add chicken stock, stirring until smooth.

Add a little water or more stock if sauce is too thick.

Put chicken pieces back into sauce and add mushrooms and artichoke hearts cut in halves.

Sprinkle lemon juice, garlic, and oregano leaves over all.

Cover and cook over low heat for 45 minutes or until tender. Add salt and pepper to taste.

Serve with rice or hot noodles.

CHICKEN & ARTICHOKE CACCIATORE

5 medium artichokes,
cooked and quartered (or
2 6-oz. jars marinated
artichoke hearts)

1 tablespoon butter

1 large chicken cut in
pieces

flour

1 large onion

1/2 pound mushrooms,
sliced

3 tablespoons olive oil (if
using fresh artichokes only)

3 cloves garlic, pressed

1/2 teaspoon oregano

1/2 teaspoon basil

1/4 teaspoon rosemary

1 to 2 pounds fresh
tomatoes (or 1 large can
tomatoes)

1/2 cup Madeira

salt and pepper to taste

Preheat oven to 350 degrees.

Put olive oil plus tablespoon butter in skillet if using fresh artichokes. If using marinated artichoke hearts, drain, putting liquid and tablespoon butter in skillet. Set artichokes aside.

Dredge chicken pieces in flour and brown in skillet until golden. Remove from skillet with slotted spoon to large casserole dish.

Add to skillet onion, mushrooms, garlic, oregano, basil and rosemary, stirring until onions and mushrooms are limp.

Add tomatoes and artichokes. Pour over chicken, spreading evenly.

Cover and bake 1 hour or until chicken is tender. During last 10 minutes of baking, add sherry and season with salt and pepper to taste.

ARTICHOKES & CHICKEN IN WINE

6 medium artichokes,
cooked
2 to 2-1/2 pounds frying
chicken pieces
7 tablespoons butter
4 carrots, cut in julienne
pieces
1/3 cup green onions, sliced
1/4 pound mushrooms,
sliced
1/4 teaspoon thyme
salt and pepper to taste
2 cups chicken broth
1 cup water
1 cup wine
4 tablespoons cornstarch

Preheat oven to 375 degrees.

Quarter artichokes and remove center petals and chokes.

In a large skillet brown chicken pieces on both sides in 5 tablespoons butter. Cover and steam chicken for 10 minutes. Remove chicken and set aside.

Add 2 tablespoons butter to skillet and sauté carrots, uncovered, 5 minutes.

Add green onions, mushrooms, thyme, and salt and pepper to taste.

Sauté 1 minute. Remove vegetables with slotted spoon and set aside.

Pour chicken broth into skillet. Stir water and wine into cornstarch and add to broth, cooking on medium heat until mixture is clear and thickened.

Arrange artichokes, chicken pieces, and sautéed vegetables in large roasting pan. Pour broth mixture over all.

Cover tightly and bake 1 hour or until chicken is tender, basting occasionally.

Carmela Meely of Walnut Creek, submitted this subtly delicious recipe to the Gilroy Garlic Festival Cook-off. She has "ripened" the artichokes and chicken with Marsala.

GARLIC CHICKEN WITH ARTICHOKES & MUSHROOMS

3/4 cup butter
8 cloves garlic, pressed
6 chicken breasts, boned and pounded flat
salt and pepper
2 tablespoons olive oil
1/4 pound mushrooms, sliced
10 small artichokes, cooked and prepared as artichoke hearts (or 1 package frozen artichoke hearts, cooked)
1 tablespoon lemon juice
1 to 2 tablespoons Marsala
1 to 2 tablespoons sherry or other white wine

In skillet melt 1/2 cup butter and add 5 cloves pressed garlic and sauté.

Add chicken breasts and sprinkle with salt and pepper. Brown, then remove chicken to warm platter.

Add 1/4 cup butter, olive oil, and 3 more cloves garlic. Brown garlic and toss in mushrooms and artichokes. Heat.

Stir in lemon juice and Marsala, sherry or other white wine. Let sauce thicken to desired consistency.

Pour over chicken. Garnish with parsley and serve with rice.

Pat Hopper of the Artichoke Advisory Board recommends highly this recipe for chicken and artichokes. She says of all the recipes she has placed in local papers, this recipe has drawn the most response.

ARTICHOKE CHICKEN SAUTÉ

2 medium artichokes
lemon juice
4 tablespoons butter
2 tablespoons water
2 chicken breasts, skinned, boned, and cut into 1/2-inch strips
1/2 teaspoon basil leaves, crushed
salt and pepper to taste
1/2 lemon
Parmesan cheese

Remove petals from artichokes until pale green petals are reached. Cut off top 2 inches of leaves, and cut dark green layer from artichoke bottoms and stems. Rub all surfaces with lemon juice.

Quarter artichokes. Remove inner leaves and chokes, then cut artichokes into thin lengthwise slices.

Sauté in 2 tablespoons butter. Add water and cook, covered, over medium heat for about 5 minutes or until water has evaporated and artichokes are tender.

Increase heat and add 2 tablespoons butter, chicken breasts, crushed basil leaves, and salt and pepper to taste.

Cook 3 to 4 minutes or until chicken is cooked.

Squeeze juice of 1/2 lemon over artichoke-chicken mix and serve with Parmesan cheese.

This is a recipe I created specifically incorporating some of our best local produce—garlic, parsley, tomatoes and artichokes. By the end of summer, canning tomatoes are very inexpensive, so I dried trays of them, filled a crock with the dried tomatoes and covered them with olive oil and garlic. They are marvelously flavorful and blend well with the chicken, artichokes, garlic and Madeira. This is a sensual recipe, worthy of serving for a special occasion. Be sure to have lots of crusty bread available to soak up the flavorful sauce.

CHICKEN POMIDORI SECCHI

3 to 4 chicken breasts, skinned, boned, and cut into bite-size pieces

1 cup onions, diced

2 cups mushrooms, sliced

12 small artichokes (about 2 inches in diameter) (or 2 packages of frozen artichoke hearts)

1 to 1-1/2 cups pomidori secchi* (or 1 3-1/2-oz. jar)

1 lemon (or 2 tablespoons vinegar)

1/4 cup fresh parsley, chopped

1/4 teaspoon dried oregano

1/4 teaspoon thyme leaves (or 4 sprigs fresh thyme and 2 sprigs fresh oregano, finely chopped)

3 to 6 large cloves garlic, minced or pressed

8 tablespoons butter

8 tablespoons olive oil

1 cup Madeira

3/4 cup heavy cream

salt and pepper to taste

FOR SERVING:

pasta for 6 to 8 servings

*To make your own pomidori secchi, see following recipe.

If using fresh artichokes remove leaves to light green-yellow leaves. Cut off stems and tops, and thinly pare the sides of the bottoms.

Cut into quarters and drop into a pot of water with the juice and rinds of 1 lemon or 2 tablespoons vinegar added.

Bring to a boil and cook until artichokes are barely tender, about 6 minutes (if using frozen artichokes, follow directions and cook until barely done). Drain and set aside.

In a large deep skillet or in a 3- to 4-quart pot, put 4 tablespoons butter and 4 tablespoons olive oil (include oil from pomidori as part of this oil and butter mixture). Melt over medium heat.

When oil and butter is hot, add chicken pieces and sauté until pink has faded and meat is barely cooked. Remove chicken from pan and place on a platter in warm oven.

Add the balance of oil and butter, and sauté onion and mushrooms until onions are translucent. Reduce heat if necessary.

Add garlic, thyme, oregano, artichokes, and tomatoes. Sauté a few more minutes, then add Madeira.

Increase heat so that Madeira will cook down, and cook about 5 more minutes or until the sauce has reduced some.

Add chicken, cream, and salt and pepper to taste, and cook a few more minutes or until piping hot.

Put freshly cooked pasta on platter and pour chicken dish over all. Sprinkle with fresh parsley, and pass Parmesan, Romano, or a mixture of both cheeses.

Serves 6 to 8.

POMIDORI SECCHI (OVEN-DRIED TOMATOES)

Wash and drain dry small, ripe tomatoes. One lug of tomatoes will fill about 6 cookie sheets with tomato halves. Italian pear-shaped tomatoes (*pomidori*) were traditionally used, but regular tomatoes work almost as well.

Remove stems, cut in half, and place cut-side up on cookie sheets or broiler pans. Lightly sprinkle with salt. Place in 175 to 200 degree oven and dry for approximately 12 hours. Check pans every few hours to rotate or to remove tomatoes that are dried. Dry until moisture has evaporated but tomatoes are not crisp.

If tomatoes appear to be browning, reduce heat. If it is difficult to dry tomatoes for that many hours consistently, dry for at least four hours, turn off heat, and continue later or the next morning.

I found there was no problem with drying the tomatoes over a 2 day period. After all, tomatoes were traditionally dried outside on racks, and nights and rainfall would interrupt the drying process.

As the tomatoes are ready, cool, then place into jars or a stoneware crock. Layer the tomatoes with olive oil (or a mixture of olive oil and salad oil), garlic cloves, and fresh or dry basil or other herbs if desired. Pack tightly. When last tomatoes are added, make certain tomatoes are covered with several inches of oil. Kept in the refrigerator, these tomatoes will keep for several months.

In addition to being a flavorful ingredient in *Chicken Pomidori Secchi*, they are delicious mixed in a cream sauce over pasta or served on a slice of baguette spread with goat's cheese or a garlic-herb cheese.

This in an excellent holiday recipe. Leftover turkey can be used in this specialty pie, or chicken, crabmeat or shrimp can be substituted. Serve with spiced peaches or apples as a condiment.

TURKEY ARTICHOKE PIE

1 bunch fresh spinach (or 1 package frozen spinach)

2 cups white or brown rice, cooked

4 tablespoons butter

10 small artichokes, cooked and prepared as artichoke hearts (or 1 package frozen artichoke hearts, thawed)

1-1/2 cups turkey, chopped

1 cup Monterey Jack cheese, shredded

1/4 pound mushrooms

2 tablespoons flour

1/2 teaspoon curry powder

1/2 teaspoon garlic powder

1 teaspoon prepared mustard

1 cup milk

salt and pepper to taste

Cook spinach, then drain well, pressing out all liquid.

Combine spinach with rice. Mix in 2 tablespoons soft butter and press rice mixture evenly over bottom and sides of well greased 9-inch pie pan.

Cover and chill up to an hour.

Preheat oven to 350 degrees.

Cut cooked artichokes into 2 to 3 pieces or blot dry packaged artichoke hearts, then cut each into 2 to 3 pieces and arrange over rice crust. Top with turkey and cheese.

In skillet over medium heat melt 2 tablespoons butter. Add mushrooms and sauté till golden.

Stir in flour, curry powder, and garlic powder, and cook until bubbly, then add prepared mustard and milk and stir until well blended. Add salt and pepper to taste.

Pour sauce over pie and bake 40 minutes or until pie is hot and cheese is bubbly.

The following recipe is a real knockout surprise for a special dinner for 2 or for a small dinner party.

BEEF OR CHICKEN WITH ARTICHOKES & BERNAISE SAUCE

Top a piece of broiled Filet Mignon or other steak with sautéed, quartered, artichoke hearts or bottoms, mushrooms, and chopped onions or shallots. Add a few spoons of *Bernaise* sauce.

If using chicken, sauté boned chicken breast, cut into 3-inch strips. Finish in the same manner as the steak.

This is nice served with a rice pilaf or thin toast points.

Pork is not often prepared with artichokes which is unfortunate as they go well together.

ARTICHOKES & PORK CHOPS WITH MUSTARD CREAM

3 large artichokes
5 loin pork chops, 1-inch thick
salt and pepper
flour
1 tablespoon oil
1-1/2 cups onions, sliced
1 to 2 cloves garlic, minced
1 cup beef bouillon
2 tablespoons wine vinegar
1 bay leaf
1 tablespoon Dijon style mustard
1 cup light cream

Preheat oven to 360 degrees.

Pull off lower outer petals of artichokes and cut off top third of artichokes. Cut in half (or quarters if artichokes are extra large). Remove center petals and chokes.

Cook artichokes in boiling water for 10 minutes. Drain.

Season pork chops with salt and pepper, and coat with flour.

In an ovenproof skillet or pan brown chops thoroughly in oil. Remove chops and drain excess fat.

Sauté onions and garlic over medium heat until golden, adding oil to pan if necessary.

Add beef bouillon, wine vinegar, and bay leaf, and bring to boil.

Place chops and artichokes in skillet, coat with juices, and bake 1 hour or until artichokes and chops are tender, basting occasionally.

Place artichokes and meat on platter and remove bay leaf from juices.

Add Dijon style mustard to pan liquids and boil until juices are reduced by half. Stir in light cream and simmer until thickened. Adjust seasonings.

Recipe can be halved; use 2 medium artichokes.

HAM & ARTICHOKE GRATIN

6 large artichokes
Bechamel sauce
1 cup Swiss cheese,
    shredded
1/2 pound mushrooms,
    finely chopped
1 tablespoon butter
1-1/2 cups cooked ham,
    finely chopped

Preheat oven to 350 degrees.

Cook artichokes and trim down to bottoms. Save leaves for other use. Arrange artichoke bottoms, cupped side up in a shallow 1-1/2-quart baking dish.

Prepare *Bechamel* sauce *(see Sauces)*, and add 1/2 cup Swiss cheese to hot sauce. Set aside.

In 10- to 12-inch frying pan, cook mushrooms in butter on medium heat, stirring until juices have evaporated, about 5 minutes.

Remove from heat and add ham and 2 tablespoons *Bechamel* sauce. Blend and mound mixture firmly on artichokes. Spoon remaining *Bechamel* evenly over tops. Sprinkle with additional 1/2 cup shredded Swiss cheese.

Bake uncovered on center rack of oven 20 minutes. Then broil, about 6 inches from heat, until top browns.

The following two recipes both use veal and are quite good. The first recipe requires a little more time than the second, however.

VEAL WITH ARTICHOKES & MUSHROOMS

8 slices of veal (about 1 pound)
1 teaspoon salt
1 teaspoon white pepper
3 tablespoons flour
1 egg
2 tablespoons water
5 tablespoons butter
1 tablespoon olive oil
2 cups artichoke bottoms, sliced
1/2 pound mushrooms, thinly sliced
2 tablespoons green onions, chopped
1 tablespoon lemon juice
1 tablespoon fresh parsley, finely chopped

Between 2 sheets of waxed paper pound veal to 1/4-inch thickness with a smooth meat mallet. Pat cutlets dry with paper towels.

Combine salt, white pepper, and flour, and dredge cutlets on both sides. Shake off excess.

Lightly beat egg with water and brush on both sides of cutlets.

In a large heavy skillet heat 2 tablespoons butter and olive oil. When hot, sauté cutlets 2 minutes on each side. As cutlets are sautéed, transfer to a heated platter and keep warm.

Heat 3 tablespoons butter and sauté artichoke bottoms, mushrooms, and green onions, stirring for about 5 minutes. Add lemon juice and parsley and cook, stirring, about 2 more minutes.

Adjust seasonings then pour over cutlets and serve immediately.

VEAL & ARTICHOKES

2 pounds veal
flour
salt and pepper
3 cloves garlic
2 tablespoons olive oil
2 tablespoons butter
1 pound fresh tomatoes
(or 1-pound can solid pack
tomatoes)
1/2 cup white wine
1/4 teaspoon oregano
leaves, crushed
1 bay leaf
24 small artichokes (or 2
packages frozen artichoke
hearts)

Prepare fresh artichokes as for hearts.

Pound veal to 1/4-inch thickness, cut in cubes, and dredge in flour seasoned with salt and pepper.

In a heavy skillet sauté garlic in olive oil and butter.

Add tomatoes, wine, oregano, and bay leaf.

Add artichokes (if using frozen, add frozen). Simmer, covered, 45 minutes or until meat is tender.

Serve over rice or pasta.

Harold Bello, a flower grower in Half Moon Bay, knew all the early artichoke growers and their families as he worked for the local bakery and traveled from farm to farm, taking orders for the crusty local bread. "All the Italians had farms growing chokes and sprouts," he recalls. "And you could always tell the families were Italian because their last names ended with 'i.' Santini, Diandi, Benedetti, Petroni, Lombardi, Consanti, Nerli, Bertolucci . . . these were the early farmers. Sure there were some whose names didn't end with 'i,' but they were the exceptions."

I later asked a Pescadero grower, Ed Campinotti, if the families with their names ending with 'i' came from a particular area of Italy, or what the connection might be with their farming artichokes and brussels sprouts. Ed looked at me, began to laugh, and said, "The way I understand it, if your name ended in 'i' you were a bastard!"

Pasta has recently gained a well deserved reputation as an Epicurean delight. No longer just the humble base for a quick, cheap dinner, pasta has become the focal point of elegant meals, dressed in unusual and delicious sauces.

The next five recipes are served with pasta. Hopefully they will provide an inspiration for experimenting with different types of pasta—fresh or dried—and with incorporating artichokes into special pasta sauces.

PASTA WITH SAUTÉED ARTICHOKES

2 large artichokes
lemon
5 to 6 tablespoons olive oil
1 cup mushrooms, sliced
1/2 cup green onions, thinly sliced
1/2 teaspoon basil
4 tablespoons white wine
salt and freshly cracked black pepper
8 oz. mostaccioli or other pasta
Parmesan cheese

Prepare artichokes as for bottoms. Peel stems. Rub all pieces with lemon. Cut into thin lengthwise slices.

In a large skillet over medium heat melt butter with olive oil. Add artichoke pieces and mushrooms. Cook 2 minutes.

Add green onion, basil, and wine. Simmer, covered, about 5 minutes or until liquid has evaporated and artichokes are tender.

Add salt and pepper to taste and serve over mostaccioli or other pasta, cooked, drained, and hot. Pass Parmesan cheese.

PASTA WITH ARTICHOKES

12 tiny fresh artichokes (or 1 package frozen artichoke hearts)

1 onion, chopped

3 tablespoons butter

2 cloves garlic, pressed or finely chopped

1/2 cup white wine

juice of 1/2 lemon

1 cup heavy cream

8 oz. fresh fettuccine, white, green or mixed

1/3 cup toasted cashews, chopped, pine nuts, or almonds

1/2 cup Parmesan cheese, freshly grated

salt and pepper to taste

Trim artichokes and prepare as for hearts, cutting in halves or quarters. (If using frozen artichokes, thaw package and use as they come from the package.)

Sauté onion in butter until the onions are translucent.

Add garlic, wine, lemon juice, and artichokes.

Cover and cook over medium heat 1 to 2 minutes.

Add heavy cream and cook, uncovered, 2 to 3 minutes longer until mixture thickens slightly.

Add fresh fettuccine, cooked, chopped nuts, and Parmesan cheese.

Toss, then add salt and freshly ground pepper to taste.

GREEN FETTUCCINE WITH ARTICHOKES & SAUSAGES

30 egg sized artichokes
3/4 pound Italian sausage
1 large onion, chopped
2 cloves garlic, pressed
1/2 cup dry white wine
2 cups chicken broth
3/4 pound green fettuccine
1/2 stick sweet butter
salt and pepper
Parmesan cheese, freshly grated
2 tablespoons fresh parsley, minced

Trim and quarter artichokes. Remove center leaves and chokes, and drop into acidulated water as they are cut.

In a large skillet sauté Italian sausage, casings removed and meat crumbled, until browned. Add onion and garlic, and cook mixture until onion is golden.

Add artichokes, wine, and chicken broth, and bring liquid to a boil.

Reduce heat, cover, and simmer the mixture 15 to 20 minutes or until artichoke hearts are just tender.

Cook mixture, uncovered, for 8 to 10 more minutes, stirring occasionally, until juices have thickened slightly. Cover and keep warm.

Cook fettuccine until it is *al dente*, drain, and transfer to heated bowl. Toss fettuccine with sweet butter.

Add artichoke mixture, and salt and pepper to taste, and sprinkle mixture with Parmesan cheese and parsley.

ARTICHOKES SIMMERED IN TOMATO VEGETABLE SAUCE WITH SPAGHETTI

4 large artichokes
1/4 cup olive oil
2 cloves garlic
1 large onion
2 carrots, shredded
4 large tomatoes (or 2 14-1/2-oz. cans tomatoes)
1/2 cup wine
1/2 teaspoon fines herbes, crushed (or 1/4 teaspoon each thyme and oregano)
salt and pepper

Quarter artichokes lengthwise. Remove center petals and chokes.

In large saucepan heat olive oil.

Add garlic, onion, and carrots, and sauté about 5 minutes or until golden.

Add tomatoes, wine, and fines herbes (or 1/4 teaspoon each thyme and oregano).

Cook until bubbly, about 2 to 3 minutes. Add artichokes and mix in well. Season to taste with salt and pepper.

Cover and simmer 10 to 15 minutes.

To serve, arrange artichoke quarters around sides of 4 soup plates. Spoon hot cooked spaghetti into center of each plate and pour sauce mixture over each serving.

CRAB & ARTICHOKE SPAGHETTI SAUCE

2 6-oz. jars marinated artichoke hearts

1/4 to 1/2 pound fresh crabmeat (or 1 can crabmeat)

16 oz. homemade meatless spaghetti sauce (or 1 bottle meatless spaghetti sauce)

1/4 cup butter

2 to 3 cloves garlic, pressed

1/2 teaspoon oregano leaves, crumbled

1/2 teaspoon thyme leaves, crumbled

1/4 teaspoon rosemary leaves, crushed

1/2 teaspoon basil leaves, crushed

spaghetti or linguine

Parmesan or Romano cheese or a mixture of both

In a saucepan heat marinated artichoke hearts and crabmeat (or 1 can king crab meat).

In another pan heat spaghetti sauce.

In third pan melt butter, garlic, oregano, thyme, and rosemary leaves.

Place cooked spaghetti or linguine on a large platter and arrange crab and artichokes alternately across top. Pour spaghetti sauce over half the dish and garlic butter over other half.

Sprinkle Parmesan/Romano cheese over top.

The following two recipes were developed by Silvana La Rocca at the Made To Order cuisine shop in Berkeley, where she is proprietor. Made To Order features fine foods, gifts, and an array of pastas to make the mouth water. The shop is spacious and airy, a very pleasant atmosphere, and the aroma of pasta and cheese is a gourmand's delight.

PASTA WITH ARTICHOKES

10 to 15 small, fresh artichokes
juice of 1 lemon
1/4 cup olive oil
salt and pepper
1 pound fresh pasta
3 eggs
1/2 to 3/4 cup parmesan cheese

Select very small, tender artichokes. Discard the tough outer leaves, cut off the stalks at the base, and trim the tips. Cut each artichoke in quarters.

Fill a 2- to 3-quart container with cold water and add lemon juice. As each artichoke is cut, place it in the lemon-water and allow to soak for about 30 minutes.

Drain the artichokes and sauté in olive oil, covered, over medium-low heat for about 10 minutes. Add salt and pepper and season to taste.

Continue to simmer, covered, over medium-low heat until the artichokes are soft and tender.

In the meantime, cook the pasta in lots of salted boiling water. While the pasta is cooking, beat the eggs with 2 to 3 tablespoons of parmesan cheese, until well blended.

When pasta is *al dente*, drain and place in a serving bowl.

Add the beaten egg mixture, the cooked artichokes, and the remainder of the parmesan cheese. Toss well and serve hot.

Serves 4 to 6.

CARCIOFINI AL DIAVOLO (DEVIL'S ARTICHOKES)

20 small, tender artichokes
4 to 6 garlic cloves, peeled
1/2 cup olive oil
1/4 cup cold water
1/4 cup fresh lemon juice
1 tablespoon hot oil, or
2 to 3 tablespoons crushed chilies

Select very small, tender artichokes. Discard tough outer leaves, cut off the stalks at the base, and trim the tops.

Gently push the leaves apart and sprinkle with salt.

In a sautée skillet cook the garlic in olive oil until the garlic is a pale blonde color.

Add the hot oil (or crushed chilies) and stir.

Add the trimmed artichokes.

Cook covered over low heat for about 5 to 6 minutes, stirring occasionally to prevent scorching.

Add lemon juice and water and continue cooking for an additional 15 to 20 minutes, or until artichokes are soft and tender.

Taste and correct for salt. Add more hot oil (or chilies) if so desired.

Serve hot or at room temperature.

Serves 4 to 6.

A number of stories are told of Catherine de Medici's influence on French food. Among the many it was said that Catherine was "scandalously" fond of artichokes. During the Renaissance artichokes were considered an aphrodisiac; consequently it was improper for a young woman to indulge in something appropriate only for men. On one occasion Catherine supposedly ate so many artichokes that a contemporary chronicler recorded that she "liked to burst."

Although no such claim can still be made for the artichoke's powers on one's prowess, it is still possible to eat them in quantity. The following three recipes for artichokes and spinach, similar but different, are good enough to lead one to excess.

SPINACH STUFFED ARTICHOKES

6 artichoke bottoms
3/4 cup Swiss or Monterey Jack cheese, grated
black olives (optional)
tarragon vinegar
FOR FILLING:
1/3 cup scallions or 1 tablespoon shallots, minced
1/2 cup melted butter
1 cup flour
1 teaspoon basil
1/8 teaspoon nutmeg
1 clove garlic, pressed
1 cup milk or light cream
1/2 cup sherry or Madeira
3 cups spinach, finely chopped, cooked
3 eggs lightly beaten
1/2 cup Parmesan or Romano cheese, grated

Preheat oven to 350 degrees.

Cook artichoke bottoms in water seasoned with tarragon vinegar.

Set bottoms, cupped side up, in shallow baking dish.

Spoon spinach filling (recipe follows) into bottoms as full as possible. Sprinkle cheese on top and garnish with black olives.

Bake 25 minutes until thoroughly heated and cheese is melted.

SPINACH FILLING:

Lightly brown scallions in butter, then slowly add flour and stir till smooth and thick.

Add basil, nutmeg, and garlic. Pour in milk or light cream, a little at a time, stirring constantly until smooth.

Add sherry and continue stirring constantly until smooth and thick. Add spinach, and stir mixture until smooth. Add eggs and Parmesan or Romano cheese and beat until smooth. Add salt and pepper to taste.

SPINACH & ARTICHOKES WITH HOLLANDAISE

8 artichoke bottoms
2 bunches fresh spinach,
    chopped (or 2 10-oz.
packages frozen chopped
    spinach)
1 cup sour cream
salt and pepper to taste
Hollandaise sauce (see
    Sauce section)

Preheat oven to 350 degrees.

Cook artichoke bottoms and place in 1-1/2-quart baking dish.

Wash and steam fresh spinach until just cooked and chop finely (if using frozen spinach thaw and drain well).

In a bowl combine spinach, sour cream, and salt and pepper to taste.

Heap spinach on top of each artichoke, cover with foil, and bake 15 minutes.

Before serving top each artichoke with *Hollandaise* sauce.

ARTICHOKE HEARTS WITH SPINACH

8 artichoke bottoms
butter
1 large bunch fresh
    spinach, chopped
6 tablespoons heavy cream
1 onion, chopped and
    sautéed in butter
salt and pepper to taste
1 cup Gruyere cheese,
    grated

Preheat oven to 325 degrees.

Sauté artichoke bottoms (either freshly cooked or bottled) lightly in butter.

Cook spinach and chop. Drain well, pressing out any residual water or juices.

Mix with heavy cream and onion, and salt and pepper to taste.

Place bottoms in casserole dish, then fill with spinach mixture. Sprinkle cheese over tops and dot with butter.

Bake until lightly browned and bubbly.

This recipe would be an excellent update on the traditional creamed onions served in many homes for Thanksgiving or Christmas. Don't wait till then, however; it would be good served with any special dinner.

ARTICHOKE & ONION STEW

24 small artichokes

2 cups water plus 2 chicken bouillon cubes (or 2 cups chicken stock)

1/2 cup dry vermouth (or dry white wine)

1/4 cup olive oil (or salad oil)

2 cloves garlic

1 teaspoon thyme leaves

1 bay leaf

1/8 teaspoon dry basil (or summer savory or oregano leaves)

24 small peeled onions

1 cup whipping cream

2 tablespoons arrowroot or cornstarch

Prepare artichokes for cooking whole.

In a 4- or 5-quart pan combine 2 cups water, vermouth (or dry white wine), olive oil (or salad oil), garlic, bouillon cubes (or substitute 2 cups chicken stock and omit the 2 cups water), thyme, bay leaf, and basil and summer savory or oregano leaves.

Bring to a boil, add onions, cover, and simmer for 15 minutes.

Add artichokes and continue cooking until artichokes are tender when pierced.

Lift vegetables from broth and set aside. To cooking broth add whipping cream mixed with arrowroot or cornstarch.

Boil rapidly, uncovered, until sauce thickens and reduces to about 1-3/4 cups, stirring frequently. Return vegetables to sauce and stir until hot.

Makes 6 first course or vegetable servings.

Each year at the Gilroy Garlic Festival there is a cooking contest. Naturally garlic is a main ingredient, but as Castroville is quite close to Gilroy, artichokes often show up in the recipes. Grand Prize for the 1983 contest went to Rosina Wilson of Albany for Artichokes a la Rosina. If you like garlic as much as you like artichokes, this is a recipe you are bound to enjoy.

ARTICHOKES A LA ROSINA

6 medium artichokes
6 large heads garlic
juice 1 large lemon
1/2 teaspoon salt
1/2 cup olive oil
FOR BAIOLI:
4 to 6 cloves garlic
2 egg yolks
1/2 teaspoon salt
3 tablespoons lemon juice
1 tablespoon Dijon style mustard
1 cup olive oil
1/2 cup basil leaves

Clean artichokes and arrange them in a large pot.

Peel off the extra papery membranes from garlic, but leave them intact. Nestle the garlic in among the artichokes.

Add water halfway up the artichokes, and squeeze in the lemon juice and tuck in the rinds. Add salt and pour olive oil over all.

Bring to a boil and simmer 45 minutes to 1 hour, depending on the size of the artichokes. Drain well.

Serve warm or cold with *Baioli* for dunking and a garnish of lemon slices and basil leaves.

Serve each diner an artichoke and a whole head of garlic which is eaten the same way the artichoke is, sort of—just pick off a clove, pull it between your teeth, and discard the skin.

BAIOLI:

Peel garlic. Place in blender container along with egg yolks, salt, lemon juice and Dijon style mustard and whirl until smooth. Add olive oil slowly, in a very thin stream, until all is incorporated. Taste for seasoning and adjust if necessary. Add basil leaves, and whirl briefly until coarsely chopped. *Baioli* is a traditional *Aioli* sauce with basil in it; for *Taioli*, add tarragon leaves, *Daioli*, add dill, and *Paioli*, add parsley.

Tom and Valerie Phipps have a ranch and produce stand in Pescadero where they specialize in organically grown produce. They are "newcomers" in the artichoke business and not Italian though Tom learned farming from Jesse Nunziati working as a farm hand on the Nunziati ranch, one of the oldest in Pescadero.

In 1969 Tom and Valerie went into the artichoke business for themselves "with 23 acres, some ancient equipment, and lots of confidence," says Valerie. "At the time lots of people told us that we could never be good artichoke farmers if we didn't have an 'i' at the end of our name, so they called us Phippseroni and Phippsi."

Despite their legitimate, English ancestry, the Phipps have done well with artichokes and other produce, often providing specialties like nastursium flowers and the tiniest artichokes for Bay Area restaurants such as Chez Panisse. Alice Waters, owner of Chez Panisse, uses many innovative and unusual California foods, including goat cheese with artichokes.

ARTICHOKE HEARTS WITH MELTED GOAT CHEESE

6 large artichokes
tarragon vinegar
1/2 cup olive oil
3/4 pound goat cheese
1 clove garlic, minced
3 sprigs thyme, stemmed and minced
pepper to taste
2 to 4 tablespoons heavy cream
1/3 cup breadcrumbs
olive oil

Preheat oven to 450 degrees.

Trim artichokes completely of leaves, stems and chokes.

Cook the artichoke hearts in boiling salted water and some tarragon vinegar for 8 to 12 minutes, depending on the size of the hearts. Test for doneness with the point of a sharp knife; the hearts should be cooked *al dente*.

Drain the artichoke hearts and marinate them while still warm in olive oil.

Trim the rind from goat cheese and mix the cheese with garlic, thyme, pepper to taste, and 2 to 4 tablespoons heavy cream. (The amount of cream will depend on the saltiness of the cheese.)

Put the artichoke hearts in a lightly oiled baking dish. Mound the mixture on them and sprinkle with bread crumbs.

Drizzle the artichokes with a little olive oil and bake them until the crumbs are completely browned and the cheese begins to melt, about 10 minutes.

A very easy dish to prepare, this is nice to serve as an accompaniment to a roast.

ARTICHOKES WITH MUSHROOMS

3/4 pound mushrooms, halved or quartered
butter
6 large artichokes, cooked and quartered (or 2 packages frozen artichokes)
1/2 teaspoon tarragon
1/3 cup cream
salt and pepper to taste

Lightly cook mushrooms in butter.

Add artichokes, cover pan, and allow to simmer 8 minutes.

Add tarragon, cream, and salt and pepper to taste.

Mix well, then turn off heat until ready to serve.

A slightly more time consuming recipe, this also makes a nice side dish, but could also be used as a vegetarian entree.

ARTICHOKES WITH MUSHROOMS

6 artichokes
8 tablespoons butter
1/4 cup green onions, finely chopped
1 pound mushrooms, halved
1/4 teaspon tarragon leaves
1/2 teaspoon marjoram leaves
2 cloves garlic, pressed
1/2 teaspoon Tabasco sauce (optional)
3/4 cup seasoned breadcrumbs
FOR CREAM SAUCE:
4 tablespoons butter
4 tablespoons flour
1 cup milk
1 cup light cream
salt and freshly ground pepper

Preheat oven to 350 degrees.

Scrape leaves and quarter bottoms of artichokes.

In a large skillet melt butter. Sauté onions until limp.

Add mushrooms, tarragon leaves, marjoram leaves, and garlic and saute 2 to 3 minutes.

Reduce heat and stir in cream sauce (recipe below) and Tabasco sauce (optional). Add artichoke scrapings and bottoms.

Pour into 1-1/2-quart casserole dish. Sprinkle with seasoned breadcrumbs and bake 25 minutes.

CREAM SAUCE:

In a saucepan melt butter over low heat. Stir in flour and cook until thick paste is formed. Remove from heat and gradually stir in milk and light cream. Return to low heat and stir constantly until thick, about 5 minutes. Add salt and freshly ground pepper to taste.

Gloria Deukmejian, wife of California governor George Deukmejian, serves *Artichokes in Wine* as an attractive and elegant side dish with roast or chops.

ARTICHOKES IN WINE

4 large artichokes
1/4 cup olive oil
3/4 cup California white wine
juice of 1 lemon
1/4 cup onion, finely chopped
1/2 teaspoon salt
1/4 teaspoon freshly ground pepper
1/4 teaspoon oregano

Cut tips off leaves and cut stems of artichokes.

Spread to open. Remove inner small leaves and choke. Place upright in a pot small enough to keep artichokes in position while cooking.

Combine olive oil, wine, lemon juice, onion, salt, pepper, and oregano, and pour into open tops of artichokes.

Boil 45 minutes or until tender, adding more wine if necessary.

Serve in a small shallow bowl, using sauce for dipping the leaves.

Moving to the undisputedly legitimate realm of eggs, this frittata recipe was entered in the Gilroy Garlic Cook-off by Fanny Cimoli of San Jose. Excellent alone, it can also be topped with a white sauce and garnished with sliced ripe olives or served on bread as a sandwich filling.

ARTICHOKE & CARROT FRITTATA

2 cups artichoke hearts, sliced or chopped, cooked
8 eggs, beaten
1 cup cheese, grated
1 cup carrot, grated
1/2 cup parsley, finely chopped
1/2 cup onion, chopped
1/8 cup celery, chopped
5 cloves garlic, pressed
1 tablespoon catsup
1 teaspoon salt
1/4 teaspoon pepper
garlic salt to taste

Preheat oven to 300 degrees.

Combine artichoke hearts, eggs, cheese, carrot, parsley, onion, celery, garlic, catsup, salt, pepper, and garlic salt to taste, and blend well.

Pour into a lightly greased 9×11-inch baking dish. Bake 20 to 30 minutes until golden brown. Do not overbake.

Cut into squares and serve.

This delightful brunch or luncheon entrée can be served hot or cold.

ARTICHOKES WITH POACHED EGGS & TART HOLLANDAISE

1 large to medium artichoke per person
1 to 2 softly poached eggs per person
FOR TART HOLLANDAISE:
3 egg yolks
3 tablespoons lemon juice
1/4 teaspoon dry mustard
1/2 cup butter, melted
1/4 cup cold butter

Trim, cook, and prepare the artichokes for stuffing, opening the leaves widely enough to make room to hold 1 or 2 softly poached eggs. The artichokes and eggs may be hot or cold.

Gently slip the eggs into the cavity and pour in about 2 tablespoons warm tart *Hollandaise,* and serve.

Pull off leaves, dipping in sauce, then with a fork beat eggs, artichoke bottom, and remaining sauce.

TART HOLLANDAISE, WARM OR COLD:

In a blender combine egg yolks, lemon juice, and mustard. Whirl at high speed for about 30 seconds, gradually pour in hot melted butter, then add cold butter, cut in small pieces (a total of 3/4 cup or 3/8 pound). Serve immediately, or cover and set aside. To rewarm, set container of sauce in warm tap water and stir occasionally. Makes about 1 cup sauce.

Substitute crabmeat or chopped ham, or add mushrooms if desired, to this recipe.

BAKED ARTICHOKE HEART & SHRIMP OMELETTE

5 eggs
1/2 teaspoon salt
1/2 teaspoon cayenne pepper
2 tablespoons olive oil
3/4 cup green onions, chopped
8 to 10 small artichoke hearts, quartered and cooked until tender (or 1 package frozen artichoke hearts, thawed and cooked 2 to 3 minutes)
1 cup shrimp, cooked and peeled
3/4 cup Jarlsburg, Monterey Jack, or Muenster cheese (or mixture)
1/4 cup Parmesan cheese

Preheat oven to 400 degrees.

In a bowl beat eggs, salt, and cayenne pepper.

In skillet heat olive oil, and sauté green onions until wilted.

Add artichoke hearts (or thawed frozen hearts), and cook 2 to 3 minutes.

Remove from heat and add shrimp. Pour artichoke mixture into eggs and blend well.

Butter a 1-1/2-quart baking dish, and pour all in. Sprinkle cheese and Parmesan cheese evenly over top.

Bake 15 to 20 minutes in upper portion of oven or until omelette is firm and knife inserted in center comes out clean.

Dina Collins, manager of the Florentine Pasta Shop in California and take out restaurant, has a recipe for a crustless artichoke quiche. Somewhere between a quiche and a frittata, it could be served for brunch or for a light entrée.

DINA COLLINS' ARTICHOKE QUICHE

1 to 2 pounds baby artichokes
4 tablespoons olive oil
1 onion, chopped
6 eggs
Parmesan cheese
1/4 cup fresh parsley, chopped
5 to 6 mushrooms, finely chopped (optional)
salt and pepper to taste

Preheat oven to 375 degrees.

Prepare baby artichokes, removing outer leaves and chokes.

Slice fine and then sauté with olive oil and onion, until artichokes are *al dente*, about 5 minutes.

Mix together eggs, a handful of Parmesan cheese, parsley, mushrooms (optional), and salt and pepper to taste. Beat well.

Combine ingredients into a non-stick pan or greased casserole and bake 20 minutes or until a toothpick inserted comes clean.

Serve warm or cold.

Another of Dolores Tottino's excellent recipes.

DOLORES TOTTINO'S ARTICHOKE QUICHE

1 medium onion, chopped
1 clove garlic, pressed
2 tablespoons butter or margarine
1/2 cup half and half
1/2 cup sour cream
1/4 cup fresh parsley, chopped
4 eggs
2 cups Swiss cheese, shredded
2-1/2 cups artichoke hearts, cooked and chopped
1-1/4 cup ham, finely chopped (optional)
salt and pepper to taste
1 9-inch unbaked pie shell

Preheat oven to 425 degrees.

Sauté onion and garlic in butter or margarine until onion is soft.

Combine half and half, sour cream, parsley, and eggs, and beat until blended.

Add onion-garlic mixture, Swiss cheese, artichoke hearts, chopped ham (optional), and salt and pepper to taste.

Mix thoroughly and pour into one 9-inch unbaked pie shell. Bake for 15 minutes at 425 degrees, then reduce to 350 degrees for 35 to 40 minutes or till set.

Cool slightly before serving.

This next recipe is my own version of a popular dish, the artichoke tart, which can be served as a main course or a delicious first course.

ARTICHOKE TART

5 large artichokes
juice and rind of 1/2 lemon
4 tablespoons butter
2 green onions, finely minced
10 to 12 sprigs parsley, minced
10 to 12 sprigs lemon thyme, chopped
2 sprigs tarragon, chopped
1 tablespoon olive oil
salt
pepper
lemon juice
2 egg yolks, lightly beaten
1 teaspoon Dijon style mustard
1/2 cup heavy cream
FOR PASTRY SHELL:
4 oz. cream cheese
1 cube butter
1 cup flour

Preheat oven to 400 degrees.

Make pastry shell (recipe below) and chill for 30 minutes or longer.

Trim artichokes to the hearts and remove the chokes. Thinly slice the artichoke bottoms and put slices in a bowl with cold water and the lemon juice and rind.

Make an herb butter by mixing 3 tablespoons softened butter with onions, parsley, lemon thyme, and tarragon.

Dry slices of artichokes and then sauté slices over medium heat in 1 tablespoon each olive oil and butter for 4 to 5 minutes. Toss the artichoke slices, still warm, with the herb butter and season with salt, fresh pepper, and a little lemon juice.

Spread the sautéed artichokes evenly in the tart shell. Pour any remaining herb butter over artichokes.

Bake tart in preheated 400 degree oven for 15 minutes. Reduce temperature to 350, leaving the oven door open for a minute to lower temperature.

Make a custard by stirring egg yolks, Dijon style mustard, and salt and pepper into heavy cream. Pour the custard mixture over the artichokes, and bake tart for about 30 more minutes, until the custard is set and golden brown.

Remove tart from oven and let stand for 20 minutes before cutting.

PASTRY SHELL:

Combine in a mixing bowl cream cheese, preferably without stabilizers added, butter, and flour. Mix well until completely blended. If mixture is very sticky or soft, chill for about 20 minutes before rolling out. Roll out on a well floured pastry cloth or board, adding a small amount of additional flour if necessary. This pastry is almost fool-proof. It isn't damaged by mixing or rolling, but be careful not to work too much additional flour into dough.

Seafood, cooked chopped chicken, turkey or ham or a combination of sautéed vegetables can be used with artichokes as other fillings for crepes. Crepes can be made ahead and frozen until used. Allow frozen crepes to come to room temperature before unwrapping and separating them.

ARTICHOKE & MUSHROOM CREPES

FOR FILLING:
6 to 8 artichoke bottoms, cooked

2 pounds mushrooms, chopped

4 tablespoons butter

1 large onion, chopped

2 cloves garlic, minced or pressed

3/4 teaspoon marjoram leaves

1/4 cup flour

3/4 cup milk

3 tablespoons dry sherry (or white wine)

1/2 cup Parmesan cheese, grated

1/4 cup parsley, chopped

salt and pepper to taste

2 tablespoons Swiss or Gruyere cheese, per crepe

FOR CREPES:
1-1/2 cups milk

3 eggs

1 cup flour

1 tablespoon oil

Preheat oven to 375 degrees.

Chop artichoke bottoms into small pieces. Scrape meat from leaves.

Remove stems from mushrooms and chop. Slice caps and set artichokes and mushrooms aside.

In a wide frying pan over medium heat, melt 2 tablespoons butter.

Add mushroom stems, onion, and garlic. Cook, stirring, until onion is limp.

Add 2 more tablespoons butter, sliced mushroom caps and artichoke pieces, and marjoram leaves. Cook, stirring, until mushrooms are soft and juices have evaporated.

Sprinkle flour over mushrooms and cook, stirring, until bubbly.

Gradually add milk and continue cooking and stirring until sauce boils and thickens. Remove from heat.

Add sherry (or white wine), Parmesan cheese, and parsley.

Let cool, then season to taste with salt and freshly ground pepper.

Fill crepes (recipe below) and place seam-side down on greased baking sheets. Bake until heated through. Before serving, sprinkle with Swiss or Gruyere cheese, and heat again about 5 minutes.

Recipe makes enough for 12 to 16 crepes.

CREPES:

In a blender or food processor, mix milk, eggs, flour and oil. Let batter rest at least 1 hour, room temperature. Heat a 6- to 7-inch crepe pan or flat bottomed pan over medium heat until hot. Grease lightly with butter. Stir batter, then pour 2 to 3 tablespoons batter all at once into center of pan, quickly tilting pan in all directions, so batter covers entire flat surface. Pour off excess if any. Cook until edge of crepe is lightly browned and surface looks dry (30 to 40 seconds). Flip gently and cook 20 seconds. If making crepes ahead, stack with a piece of waxed paper between each crepe. Package airtight and refrigerate for up to 3 days. Allow crepes to come to room temperature before separating. Fill on side that isn't browned.

The following Spanish recipe is somewhat reminiscent of *Paella*. Add 1/2 teaspoon saffron threads to the rice mixture to create that classic flavor.

BAKED ARTICHOKES BARCELONA STYLE

1/3 cup onion, chopped
1/3 cup green pepper, chopped
1 clove garlic, minced
2 tablespoons olive oil
3/4 cup boned chicken, cut in small pieces
3/4 cup bulk sausage pieces
3/4 cup uncooked rice
1 14-oz. can chicken broth (or 14-oz. soup stock)
1/2 cup peas
1 tomato, peeled and chopped
4 large artichokes, cooked

Preheat oven to 350 degrees.

Sauté onion, green pepper, and garlic, in olive oil until onion is tender.

Add boned chicken and sausage pieces (or use 1-1/2 cups of either chicken or sausage).

Cook and stir until browned. Drain off excess fat.

Stir in uncooked rice. Cook and stir 2 minutes.

Add chicken broth (or stock). Simmer, covered, 20 minutes.

Stir in peas and tomato. Cook, covered, 10 more minutes.

Remove centers and chokes of artichokes and stuff with rice mixture.

Place in baking dish; add 1/2 inch water. Bake uncovered about 15 minutes or until filling is thoroughly heated.

H.G. Glasspoole, in the History of Our Common Cultivated Vegetables, *1875, says of artichokes, "Medicinally the stalks are considered aperient and diuretic. The leaves in their natural state, boiled in white wine whey, are thought beneficial in the case of jaundice; and when cut into pieces and steeped in sherry wine, are an excellent anti-billious medicine."*

Apparently Glasspoole was accurate, or at least convincing, as there are several medicines produced in Argentina to treat the liver and billiousness that are made with artichokes as the active ingredient.

The next five recipes have a definite Eastern flavor to them, all coming from or having been adapted from, recipes of Eastern Europe and Central Asia.

This first hearty recipe, adapted from the *Moosewood Cookbook* by Mollie Katzen, would make a very nice side dish with lamb, but is quite substantial as a main dish on its own. This recipe can be doubled.

PILAF STUFFED ARTICHOKES

6 medium artichokes
FOR FILLING:
2-1/2 cups cooked (or 1-1/4 cups raw) brown rice
2 scallions, chopped
1 to 2 teaspoons dried mint
juice from 1 lemon
1/4 cup fresh parsley, chopped
1/4 cup toasted pinenuts, chopped (or 1/2 cup toasted and chopped almonds)

Preheat oven to 350 degrees.

Cook artichokes and prepare for stuffing, removing center leaves and chokes.

Fill with the pilaf and bake, covered, until heated through, about 20 minutes.

Serve topped with Feta cheese, Greek lemon-egg sauce (see *Sauce* section) or a dollop of yogurt or sour cream.

FILLING:

Rice, scallions, mint, lemon juice, parsley, and toasted pinenuts (or 1/2 cup toasted and chopped almonds).

ARTICHOKES STUFFED WITH LAMB & WHEAT

4 large artichokes
1/2 cup cracked wheat
2 tablespoons olive oil
2/3 cup onion, chopped
1 pound ground lamb
2 cloves garlic, minced
1/3 cup pinenuts (or almonds), chopped
2 teaspoons fresh mint, minced
1/2 teaspoon thyme leaves
1/4 cup white wine
salt and pepper to taste

Preheat oven to 350 degrees.

Cook artichokes until tender.

Remove tough outer leaves and prepare for stuffing.

While artichokes are cooking, pour 1 cup boiling water over cracked wheat. Let stand until tender, about 1/2 hour.

In olive oil, sauté onion, ground lamb, garlic, and pinenuts (or almonds) until meat is browned.

Add mint, thyme leaves, and salt and pepper to taste.

Add wine and cook another 3 to 4 minutes.

Mix in cracked wheat and stuff into artichokes. Bake 10 to 15 minutes or until thoroughly heated.

Serve with melted butter or Greek lemon-egg sauce.

The flavors and spices used in Eastern cooking often taste strange to Western palates. Exposure to methods of preparing foods, however, can really expand culinary opportunities. The following recipe is similar to Indian recipes using potatoes and vegetables, in this case, artichokes. In the original recipes there were several steps to preparing the vegetables. I have simplified this to be more in keeping with Western schedules.

ARTICHOKE & POTATOES IN OIL & LEMON

4 fresh medium to large artichokes
lemon half
1 large potato
1 large onion
3 tablespoons lemon juice
1/2 cup olive oil
butter
1 teaspoon whole fennel seeds (or 3 pieces star anise)
2 teaspoons whole coriander seeds (or 1/2 cup fresh coriander leaves)
2 bay leaves
4 cloves garlic, peeled and slightly mashed
salt to taste

Prepare artichokes as for artichoke bottoms. Quarter and rub all parts of the artichokes with a half of a fresh lemon.

Peel potato and cut into sections roughly the same size as artichoke pieces. Peel onion and cut into 8 sections.

Tie fennel, coriander, bay leaves, and garlic into a cheesecloth bundle and put into a 2-1/2-quart pot.

Add 2 cups of water and bring to a boil.

Add lemon juice, olive oil, and salt to taste. Put artichoke, potato and onion pieces into prepared liquid and bring to boil again.

Cover, lower heat, and simmer about 12 minutes. Check vegetables for tenderness. Correct seasonings and cook until fork tender.

Remove cover and allow vegetables to cool in liquid.

Remove vegetables with slotted spoon and serve with butter.

MIDDLE EASTERN LAMB & ARTICHOKES

8 medium artichokes
2 pounds boneless trimmed lamb
flour
1/4 cup olive oil
1 onion, chopped
1/2 teaspoon thyme
3 cloves garlic, minced
4 cups broth or soup stock
lemon juice
salt and pepper

Cook artichokes until barely tender. Drain and cool. Prepare as for artichoke hearts and cut in quarters.

Cut lamb into small cubes and roll in flour.

In heavy frying pan or Dutch oven, sauté lamb in olive oil until browned on all sides.

Add onion and when lightly browned, sprinkle with 1 tablespoon flour. Stir until blended.

Add thyme and garlic.

Add broth (made from lamb bones or chicken) and cook, covered, 20 minutes.

Adjust seasonings and add artichoke hearts.

Cover and cook until tender, adding lemon juice, salt, and freshly ground pepper to taste.

Serve over cracked wheat with sour cream or yogurt on side.

The following Syrian recipe is quite spicy but not at all hot. A very unique dish.

SYRIAN ARTICHOKES

6 large artichokes
1-1/2 pounds lamb
2 tablespoons olive oil
2 tablespoons butter
2 medium onions, chopped
1/2 cup celery, sliced
1/4 teaspoon cumin
1/4 teaspoon curry powder
1/4 teaspoon pepper, freshly ground
1/8 teaspoon cinnamon
1/8 teaspoon allspice
salt to taste
2 6-oz. cans tomato sauce
3/4 cup orange juice
1 teaspoon soy sauce

Preheat oven to 325 degrees.

Cook artichokes about 20 minutes. Drain.

When cool, remove small tough outer leaves and prepare for stuffing. Place cupped side up in a baking dish.

Cut lamb into small cubes and sauté in olive and butter with onions until onions are limp and golden.

Add celery and continue cooking about 5 more minutes.

Add cumin, curry powder, freshly ground pepper, cinnamon, allspice, and salt to taste.

Combine tomato sauce, orange juice, and soy sauce.

Set aside 3/4 cup sauce and reserve. Mix the balance of the sauce with the meat mixture and cook 15 more minutes. Stuff into artichokes. Pour remaining sauce over artichokes.

Bake about 45 minutes or until meat and artichokes are tender.

A good Indian recipe, this one incorporates artichokes with spinach and lamb and uses ginger and turmeric for spices. This recipe was probably an adaptation of a Central Asian recipe, passed on through family or by a traveler.

SAG GOSHT

2 pounds lamb shoulder or
leg, boneless
1/4 cup flour
3 tablespoons oil
1 cup onion, finely chopped
3 cloves garlic, pressed
20 oz. spinach, chopped
and cooked
2 cups artichoke bottoms,
sliced
1 teaspoon ground ginger
1/2 teaspoon turmeric
salt and pepper to taste

Cut lamb in 1-inch cubes and dredge in flour. Shake off excess.

In a Dutch oven or heavy pot heat oil and brown lamb on all sides in small batches. As lamb browns, remove with slotted spoon.

In same pot sauté onion, stirring 3 mintues. Add garlic, and sauté about 2 more minutes.

Return lamb to pot. Add spinach, artichoke bottoms, ginger, turmeric, and salt and pepper to taste, and mix well.

Reduce heat to simmer, cover, and cook 30 minutes.

Serves 6.

ADDITIONAL IDEAS FOR HOT DISHES

Add artichoke hearts or bottoms to a favorite recipe for *Beef Stroganoff* or stew for a delightful variation of an old favorite. If using marinated artichoke hearts, use the marinade when sautéeing the mushrooms and onions. The marinade will add zest to the sauce.

When making baked fish, pour the marinade from a jar of artichoke hearts over fish before baking. Add artichoke hearts, coarsely chopped, with finely chopped green onions and minced parsley a few minutes before fish is completely cooked.

Enchiladas, either cheese, meat or seafood, are enhanced by adding chopped artichoke hearts or bottoms.

Add fresh or marinated artichoke hearts to a homemade pizza for an original and delicious addition to other pizza toppings.

Frozen artichoke hearts or small fresh artichoke hearts are a delicious addition to skewered meats or vegetables either barbecued or prepared as shish kebab or Japanese style. Marinate artichokes along with other foods before cooking.

Add artichoke hearts to *Seafood Newberg* or *Oysters Rockefeller* for California style seafood. Artichoke hearts are always a welcome addition to scrambled eggs or omelettes; use white cheese such as Jarlsberg or Gruyere for an especially delicious omelette.

Because of their distinct but mild flavor, artichokes can be used in most entrée and side dish recipes; they add a little elegance and specialness to what might otherwise be an everyday meal.

*They sometimes Broil the Artichoaks, and as the
Scaly leaves open, baste them with fresh and
sweet Oyl; but with Care extraordinary, for if a
drop fall upon the Coals, all is marr'd that
hazard escap'd, they eat them with the Juice of
Orange and Sugar.*

Evelyn on Italian Artichoke Cookery

DESSERTS

Unless artichokes are abundant and inexpensive, desserts made with artichoke pulp can be expensive to prepare. If experimentation interests you, or a very unusual and special dessert is needed, here are a few recipes that are bound to please. Also, artichoke pulp can be substituted for applesauce in a spice cake, and pulp can be used in fruitcake—about 2 cups per recipe would be the correct measurement. If artichokes are available at a reasonable price, use your imagination.

ARTICHOKE NUT BREAD

3/4 cup milk
1 cup artichoke pulp
1 egg
1/4 cup butter
2-1/2 cups flour
3/4 cups sugar
2 teaspoons baking powder
1 teaspoon baking soda
1 teaspoon cinnamon
1 teaspoon nutmeg
1/2 teaspoon salt
1/2 teaspoon ginger
1 cup walnuts, chopped

Preheat oven to 350 degrees

Melt the butter and in a small bowl combine milk, artichoke pulp, egg, and butter.

In another bowl mix together flour, sugar, baking powder, baking soda, cinnamon, nutmeg, salt, and ginger. Add walnuts.

Add to milk mixture and blend only until dry ingredients are moistened.

Pour into 2 4×8-inch loaf pans, lightly greased. Bake 55 minutes.

Serve warm with butter or chilled, sliced thin, with cream cheese spread.

DOLORES TOTTINO'S ARTICHOKE CAKE

3/4 cup sour milk (or cream)
3/4 cup artichoke pulp
1/2 cup butter
1/2 cup white sugar
3/4 cup brown sugar
2 eggs
2 cups sifted flour
2 teaspoons baking powder
1 teaspoon baking soda
1 teaspoon cinnamon
1/2 teaspoon ginger
1/2 teaspoon allspice
1/2 teaspoon salt (optional)
1/2 cup walnuts
1/2 cup raisins
1/2 teaspoon vanilla

Preheat oven to 325 degrees.

Grease and flour a 7×11-inch baking pan and side aside.

In a small bowl combine sour milk (or cream) and artichoke pulp. Set aside.

In another bowl cream butter and sugars. Add eggs and beat well, about 3 minutes.

In large bowl mix sifted flour, baking powder, baking soda, cinnamon, ginger, allspice, and salt (optional). Add walnuts and raisins.

Combine alternately dry ingredients with milk-pulp mixture and butter mixture, mixing well. Add vanilla.

Place in prepared baking pan and bake 45 minutes or until top springs back when tested.

Linda Pesce, a Castroville area grower's wife, wrote an article for *Farm Wife News* titled "The Beach Life with Artichokes." In her article she offers some artichoke variations of classic recipes:

> *I have also used artichoke pulp just as you would use applesauce to make an applesauce cake, resulting in an artichoke cake. Another unusual recipe is to make an artichoke pie, using artichoke pulp from the heart the same as you would use pumpkin to make a pumpkin pie. I flavor it about the same as a pumpkin pie.*

ARTICHOKE FESTIVAL

CASTROVILLE
THE ARTICHOKE CENTER
OF THE WORLD

CASTROVILLE
Artichoke Festival
FRENCH FRIED
ARTICHOKES

AFTERCHOKE

ARTICHOKE ETIQUETTE

Artichokes are a true finger food. Pull the leaves off, one at a time, dip the tender, fleshy end into a sauce or dip, and draw the fleshy end through the front teeth, scraping off the inside edible part.

When the purple-tipped cone of the light leaves is reached, take a spoon and scoop them and the *choke* or thistle out, and discard. The remaining portion is called the *bottom* or *heart*, otherwise known as *the best part*. Fill the heart or dip it into the sauce and eat slowly, savoring the delicate flavor of the artichoke.

A recent letter received by the California Artichoke Advisory Board and the Board's response might provide some insight on leaf-eating etiquette:

> *Gentlemen:*
>
> *For a number of years I have been involved in an argument with family and friends as to the proper method of eating artichokes. The question is . . . do you scrape the meat off the petals with your upper teeth or your lower teeth? I would like to know the Board's official position on this so that we can put this to rest. Your article in the Christian Science Monitor was good but would have been better if the official position on scraping the petals had been included.*
>
> *Please let me know as soon as possible since there is not too much time left in Artichoke Season.*
>
> *Sincerely,*
> *A Concerned Artichoke Eater*

Dear Concerned Eater,

Thank you for your recent letter requesting our official position on how to correctly eat an artichoke. The Artichoke Advisory Board has been very remiss in dealing with this area of artichoke etiquette. We have been involved in an informal research study regarding just this issue, but our results are sketchy as we have been gathering the data for only the past ten years. To date the data are:

If you are afflicted with an overbite (250) the recommendation is to scrape using the lower teeth. Those with an underbite (47), should use the upper teeth. If you have artificial teeth (14), the recommendation is to use the upper plate for scraping to reduce drag on the lower teeth. However, a member of the American Dental Association (1), recommends that you alternate between the upper and lower teeth to reduce wear and tear on the teeth.

If you would like to be a part of our research study, please send us information on your preferences.

Sincerely,
The Artichoke Advisory Board

A WORD ON
ARTICHOKES & WINE

During the 1960's there was sentiment among some gourmands that artichokes should *never* be served with wine, the reason being that the subtle, delicate flavor is lost in the overpowering quality of wine. Artichokes were often served as the first course of a meal so that wine could be served after.

This feeling was certainly not shared by those of Mediterranean, North African, or Central Asian heritage. The early California coastal farmers made hearty red wine on their farms (though the grapes came from the inland valleys), and red wine accompanied all foods. Although many Italian families now drink white wine with artichokes, a number of families still hold tightly to the feeling that red is best.

Sotere Torregian suggests that red wine from the Georgian Soviet People's Republic is the correct wine to serve as it has "very ancient links with the Mediterranean and Armenian civilizations as well as Arab traditions." He also suggests red Greek *Retsina* or Lebanese *Araq* (anise) liquor.

Both Ron Duarte of Duarte's Tavern and Horace Mercurio of the Moss Landing Oyster Bar and Company recommend the Chardonnays, Sauvignon Blanc, Fume Blanc or Dry Reislings for white wines and Petit Sirah or Zinfandel for the red wines.

My suggestion, certainly backed by most specialists on wine, is to experiment. Prepare a few artichoke dishes some lazy afternoon and invite friends to bring their favorite wines. An artichoke and wine tasting party could be an excellent way to celebrate the return of warm weather as well as a pleasant way to entertain and enjoy the pleasures of artichokes and wine.

There is also an alcoholic beverage made from artichokes, designed to be served as an appetizer. *Cynar,* as it is known, is made and served in Italy, Argentina, and probably Chile as well. It is a strong, bitter drink that is served straight or with soda or vermouth and poured over ice. It is quite popular with the old-time growers and a few others who have acquired a taste for the bitter flavor. As some countries consider the artichoke to be a stomach sedative, *Cynar* is perhaps ideal for the purpose. If you can hold it down it likely fortifies the stomach for an evening of serious eating, especially if the capability of the cook is in question.

FOR KIDS, TOO!

Artichokes are a marvelous food to serve to children. Eaten with the fingers, artichokes are almost a play food—easy to handle and fun to dip into mayonnaise or sauce. And because artichokes are plentiful in vitamins and minerals, they have the additional advantage of being a healthy food.

My daughter enjoyed artichokes as soon as she was old enough to grasp the concept of eating the ends of the leaves. For several years, however, she wanted nothing to do with the heart or bottom of the artichoke (something I didn't mind because I got to eat it for her). Then finally, when she was about 5, she mustered her courage, ate one, and has never passed one up since. It turns out that the word "heart" had worried her as she associated it with her heart, and it seemed a terrible thing to eat the artichoke's heart.

A nice way to introduce children to artichokes is to present them with one boiled or steamed until tender, cooled to room temperature, and perhaps spread open to make it almost flower-like in appearance. Serve a small dish of mayonnaise or melted butter on the side. Demonstrate how to eat the ends of the leaves, letting them know that after eating the leaves they will come to a little cup that tastes just like the leaf-ends. (This circumvents the potential stand-off with the "heart.")

The recipe for the artichoke sunflower is also an excellent way to introduce artichokes to children. The hot sauce and shrimp could be eliminated or substituted with shelled sunflower seeds. Children could even apply the cream cheese spread to the leaves. I have found that children are more likely to try foods they have prepared themselves than those that are simply served to them.

French fried artichoke hearts might be a good way to introduce artichokes to a truly finnicky eater. I had a cousin who subsisted mainly on peanut butter sandwiches and Hydrox cookies but who thoroughly enjoyed a plate of zucchini that my mother had cunningly disguised by french frying it. The crunchy, slightly sweet taste of the fried hearts should indeed melt the hearts of even the most determined non-vegetable eaters.

GROWING YOUR OWN

*The stalke bringeth forth on the top a fruit like a globe,
resembling at first a cone or pineapple, that is to say, made up of
many loose scales; which is, when the fruit is great or loosed, of
a greenish red colour within, and in the lower part full of
substance and white; but when it opens it selfe, there growes also
upon the cone a floure all of threads, of a gallant purple tending
to a blew colour.*

Early writer describing the artichoke plant's flowerbuds

Artichoke plants make a beautiful addition to a garden, both as a food crop and as an ornamental. The silvery-green fronds are almost fern-like, and if the buds are allowed to mature, the other-worldly purple-blue flowers are show stoppers.

Although the plant may take up to a year to produce its first crop, in mild weather locations it is a perennial and will require little work once producing. It will continue to produce for 5 to 8 years or longer before needing to be divided and replanted. Depending upon the climate artichoke plants can be good food producers, an ornamental, or a pampered plant requiring a lot of attention. However, if you are a true artichoke devotee it may well be worth the extra work to produce a crop at home.

The ideal artichoke climate is the California coastal fog-belt. The cool, mild weather allows for a long producing season (September to May), and the plants require minimum care. In any area where the weather is warm and sunny and the winter temperatures seldom fall below 30 degrees, the plants will also grow well.

The season for *quality* artichokes is short, however, as the summer heat causes the buds to mature too quickly, and winter frosts will slow down growth. In Louisiana, for instance, the *Creole* artichoke grows quite well, but it only produces a good crop in the spring. In areas where winters are cooler, edible buds will be ready at the beginning of summer.

In mountainous areas or places where winter temperatures are cold, the plants have a more difficult time. They do all their growing from early spring to the first heavy frosts, which allows little time to produce buds and flowers. They must also be well protected to survive winter.

March is the primary planting month for artichoke plants, though along the California coast plants are set anytime from December through May. In other areas plants can be put in the ground as early as February or as late as April, depending on the climate. If the ground is too cold, the unprotected roots could freeze, but if planted too late, some of the valuable growing season is lost.

Along the coast, artichoke plants receive sun all day. In warmer climates the plants do better with a half day of shade. Don't plant artichokes under a tree to get shade, however. Artichokes don't do well if they have to compete for water and nutrients. Placing plants near a lawn that receives regular food and water would be excellent. Artichokes prefer heavy, rich soil that drains well; standing water or poor drainage will cause root rot. Because artichokes are perennials, make certain the soil is rich and full of nutrients before planting.

Artichokes are grown from a stump, a piece of root stalk that has been cut from an established plant. Bare root stalk divisions are sold in coastal nurseries from late December through the spring. Root divisions are the most reliable method of growing artichokes but are not as vigorous as seeds. For this reason gardeners in cold climates often grow plants from seeds. The seeds can be purchased in cell packs and occasionally in larger containers. Plants grown from seeds will not be as consistent in shape and size as those grown from stumps and may even produce only inedible thistles. If this happens, however, you still have an ornamental crop with flowers that can be sold for more than $3.00 each.

The larger the seedling or root division when planted, the more productive the plant will be in its first year. To plant from root stock, place the stump in the ground in a vertical position with the base of any new shoots just above ground. Allow approximately 4 feet spacing in all directions. If using artichoke plants as a border or hedge, they can be placed slightly closer together, but they tend to spread out as they grow. Water heavily after planting.

Seeds should be sown indoors or in a greenhouse about 2 months before the late frosts. Refrigerate seeds for 2 weeks before sowing to help insure sprouting. Seedlings will be ready to be planted when they are 4 to 6 inches high.

Keep plants as weed-free as possible, as weeds pull needed water and nutrients from plants. Water once a week or more often if necessary, especially in the summer.

Insect problems may occur, aphids being the most likely pest. Hose plants down well with a strong blast of water. Malathion can be used, but don't use it for at least 1 to 2 weeks before harvest. If gophers plague your garden, wrap the roots in wire mesh before planting.

In mild climates feed the plants with a complete fertilizer after the last of the spring harvest. Plants can be fed 2 to 3 times a year to promote vigorous growth. In cold winter areas, feed plants in the spring after you have uncovered them. Plants grown in desert areas may become dormant in the summer. Regardless, mulch all plant roots to keep them cool.

Coastal farmers often cut the entire plant to the ground after the spring harvest to produce a bigger fall crop. On some ranches plants are cut at different times of the year to extend the harvest season. Cutting back the plants is recommended only for mild-winter/cool-summer areas.

The artichoke growing on the central stalk will mature first and will be the largest on the plant. This bud may grow to more than 4 inches in diameter. Buds on the side stalks will be ready soon after and will be somewhat smaller. They will be tough if allowed to grow as large as the central bud. The tiny buds near the base of the plant are the "hearts." They should be harvested at 1-1/2 to 2 inches in diameter and used for dishes calling for "artichoke hearts."

The younger the bud is when picked the more tender it will be. Buds picked at full size have the most flavor, so it is important to pick them when they are full-sized, but before the bracts have opened. Buds maturing in the late winter or spring are usually tightly closed and very fleshy.

Summer and fall buds will be looser. Pick these when they are as tight as possible, even if it means sacrificing some of the flavor. Plants will produce more buds if the harvested buds are small, thus increasing production time. Once the plant begins to flower, bud production will slow down.

After a stem has finished producing, it will appear to fold up and will begin to die back. Cut the stems to the base of the plant. New foliage will appear in a short period of time.

In cold winter areas, cut back old foliage and stems before the first heavy frosts. Cover the plant crown with leaves. Next, pile about a foot of loose mulch and straw over the plant. For extra protection, place a wooden box over the mulched plant. Another technique is to place 4 stakes around the plant, then wrap it in polyethylene film. After the danger of heavy frost has passed, remove the protective materials and feed the plants.

If the ground is still likely to freeze, dig up the stumps and store them in a frost-free place. You can also grow the plant as an annual, replanting new seedlings or stumps each spring.

Three to four plants will produce enough buds for a small family. The center midribs on the young stalks can also be eaten. They should be cut into 6 inch lengths, blanched and peeled, then prepared by steaming or sauteeing just until tender.

Artichoke plants can also be grown in containers. The soil needs to be rich and not compacted, in containers large enough to allow the roots to expand.

A word to the wise for home growers: My brother discovered that insects, mice, gophers, and humans are not the only artichoke fans. He lives in the Santa Cruz mountains and one year was patiently waiting for his artichoke buds to mature. Just before harvest, one of his German Shepherds escaped from her kennel and paid a midnight visit to the garden. She ate approximately 50 artichokes, biting the buds off at the stems and then eating the succulent hearts.

Raccoons, deer, and goats are also quite fond of the flowerbuds, which seems to prove Pliny wrong, who in a treatise on artichokes, concluded by chastising his fellow countrymen for serving a food that asses and other beasts refuse for fear of prickling their lips.

WHERE TO START

California coastal residents can purchase root stumps at most nurseries, especially in the area between Half Moon Bay and Monterey. Many inland nurseries will carry them also. Request that your nursery obtain stumps, or inquire about local nurseries that will have them in the spring.

Recommended seed packs are:

Grande Beurre (on some seed racks) and *Green Globe* (order from W. Atlee Burpee Co., Warminster, PA 18974; or from Thompson & Morgan, Box 1808, Jackson, N.J. 08527).

An excellent sourcebook for finding seeds for artichokes as well as for many other vegetables (and fruits) is *The Seed Finder*, by John Jeavons & Robin Leler (this book can be ordered directly from the publisher: Ten Speed Press, P.O. Box 7123, Berkeley, CA 94707; $5.95 postpaid).

For more information about growing artichokes, contact the California Artichoke Advisory Board, P.O. Box 747, Castroville, CA 95012 (408) 633-4411.

THE CASTROVILLE
ARTICHOKE FESTIVAL

In September the brown hills to the east of Castroville reflect the long, dry California summer. All is sunburned except the spreading dark green oak trees that dot the hills. Small groups of cattle graze on the slopes. Castroville lies over the hills at the edge of the coastal plain which stretches away to the west. This is the season for the Artichoke Festival.

The Castroville Artichoke Festival began in 1959 with a parade and community barbeque under the sponsorship of the Castroville Rod and Gun Club and the Phil Marinovich Marching Units. Traditionally a three-day affair, the festival begins on a Friday night in early September (usually the weekend following Labor Day), opening with a dinner and the selection and crowning of the new Artichoke Queen. A dance follows.

Highlights of Saturday's activities are the 10-K Race, Arts and Crafts Fair, Antique Market Place, and continuous music and entertainment. Sunday morning starts with a fire house pancake breakfast. This is followed at 10 AM by the parade.

For more information on the festival, you can contact:
CASTROVILLE ARTICHOKE FESTIVAL
P.O. Box 1041
Castroville, CA 95012
(408) 633-CHOK

THE ARTICHOKE
ADVISORY BOARD

The Artichoke Advisory Board is the promotional arm of the artichoke industry and an informational clearinghouse. For more information on the artichoke industry or on artichokes in general, please contact:

ARTICHOKE ADVISORY BOARD
P.O. Box 747
Castroville, CA 95012
(408) 633-4411

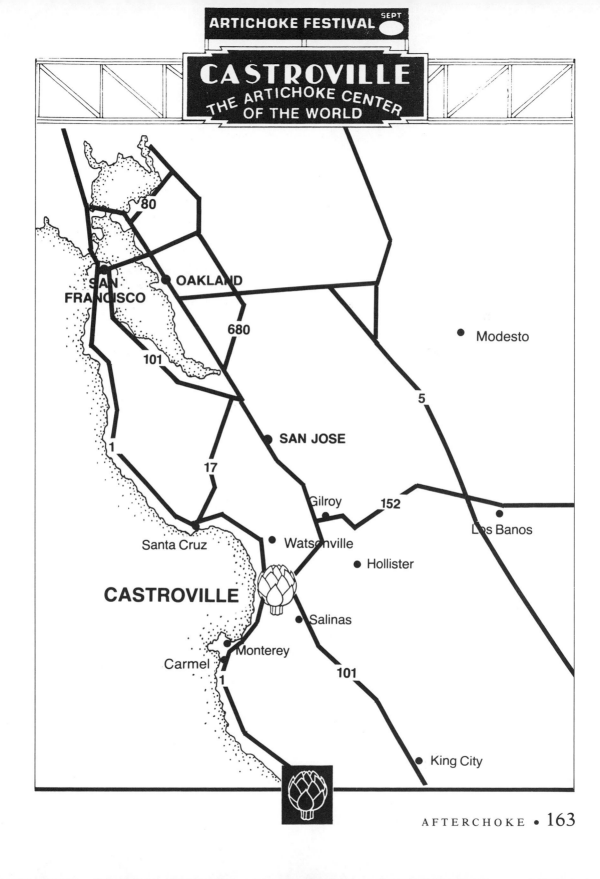

INDEX

ABOUT
BATISTA MOON STUDIOS
& THE FRONT COVER
OF THIS BOOK

The exotic cross-section of an artichoke which decorates the cover of this book is an image created by artists Barbara & Fernando Batista at Batista Moon Studio in Monterey. The image was originally developed for the Castroville Artichoke Festival, and is available as a beautiful 6-color poster (see details below).

Batista Moon Publishing began in 1980 with the Monterey Jazz Festival Poster. Since then, they have continued to develop posters which have received widespread public and critical acclaim, have appeared on covers of several prestigious journals and magazines, and have been included in the permanent collection of posters in the *Musée De L'Affiche* in Paris.

THE CASTROVILLE ARTICHOKE FESTIVAL POSTER is available directly from Batista Moon Studio. The poster measures 20″×28″, and is in 6 colors with 2 varnishes. The cost is $15.00 plus tax and $5.00 for handling and shipping via UPS. Visa, Mastercharge, American Express or personal cheques accepted. Please send your order directly to:

BATISTA MOON STUDIO
444 Pearl Street
Monterey, CA 93940
(408) 373-1947

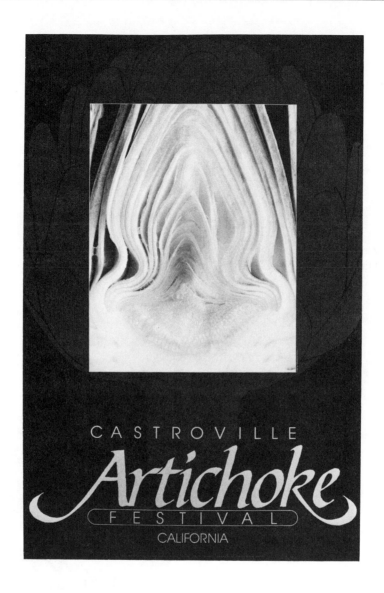

CASTROVILLE

Artichoke

FESTIVAL

CALIFORNIA